Copyright Wilhelm 2024

Email: wilhelm@wilhelmbooks.co.za
https://wilhelmbooks.co.za

Cover Design and Illustrator: Linta Anish ~ linsaraillustration

Sakura Book Publishing, Durban, South Africa
www.sakurabookpublishing.com
alta@sakurabookpublishing.com

ISBN: 978-1-0370-2687-4(print)
978-1-0370-1-0370-2688-1(e-book)

All rights reserved. No part of this publication may be reproduced, distributed, or transmitted in any form or any means, including photocopying, recordings, or other electronic or mechanical methods without the prior written permission of the author, except in the case of brief quotations embodied in critical reviews and certain noncommercial uses permitted by copyright law.

## DISCLAIMER

This work is inspired by real events and people, but it has been fictionalized for creative purposes. Names, characters and details have been changed to protect privacy and enhance the narrative. Any resemblance to actual persons, living or dead, or actual events is purely coincidental and not intended by the author.
The author and publisher make no claims to the accuracy of events or the portrayal of characters and are not liable for any misinterpretation. This story is provided "as is" and any opinions expressed are those of the characters and do not reflect the views of the author or publisher.

# From Hippie to Preacher
## Wilhelm

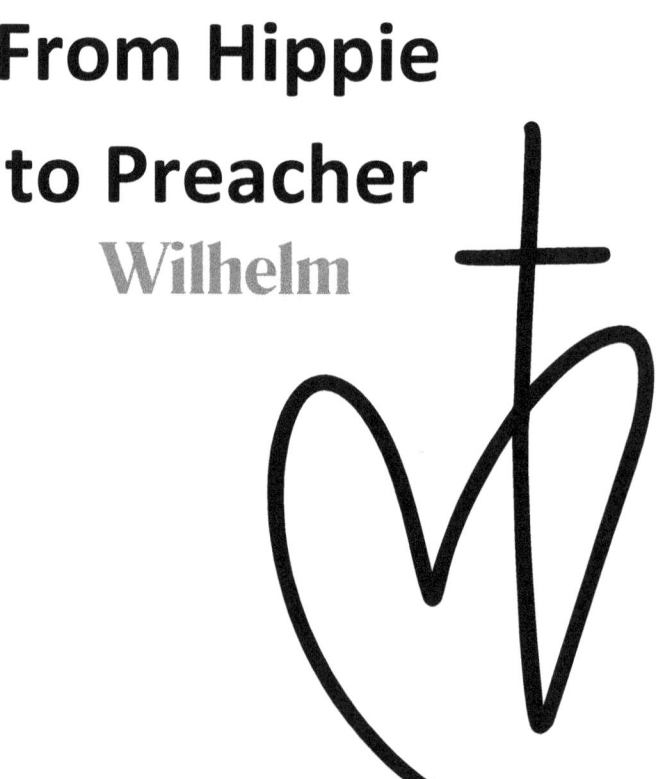

# Wilhelm

Born in Windhoek, where the vast desert winds whisper stories of resilience, the author's early years were steeped in the open skies and rugged landscapes of Namibia.

But it was the old Western Transvaal, where he grew up and studied, that truly shaped the man he would become. There, beneath the endless sun, life was a mix of tradition and quiet determination—qualities that would later echo in his writing.

*From Hippie to Preacher*

Growing up in the early '50s and '60s wasn't easy, especially in a house bustling with six children and a father who worked deep in the mine. I was the eldest, which, though it might sound like a small thing, was a title that carried weight—more than my skinny shoulders often cared to bear. Being the eldest meant I was the one to make sure there was enough chopped wood and that a bucket of coal sat ready beside the big, black stove before I left for school each morning. The fire had to be hot before the first crack of dawn, heating the house from its cold bones, because without it, there was no warmth at all. We didn't have an electric stove like some of the families in town. Ours was a hulking coal stove.

Once a week, like clockwork, the coal truck made its rounds through the rows of houses, a

*From Hippie to Preacher*

lumbering giant, spitting black smoke and rumbling down the street like a mechanical beast. Everyone in the neighbourhood knew its sound, knew what it brought—a lifeline of fuel that kept the hearths burning. The driver would holler from the cab, and we'd scramble out to meet him, muddy boots crunching against the gravel. Our weekly order was always the same: two bags of coal, and one bag of wood. The coal came in rough, burlap sacks, each one weighing more than I could lift without grunting. I'd drag them as best I could, careful not to tear the sacks, while my younger brothers and sisters huddled near, watching with wide eyes as the wood was stacked. There was no room for laziness in those days, not when the mornings bit with frost and the evenings stretched long and cold. The coal and wood didn't just keep the stove alive—it kept us alive.

*From Hippie to Preacher*

That stove was the heart of our home, a constant companion in the kitchen, its fire glowing orange through the grate, casting shadows that danced on the walls as we ate our supper. I can still see it now, that warm flicker, lighting up the lines on my father's face as he came in from a hard day's work. He'd glance at the stove, then at me, a silent nod of approval passing between us. We understood each other in a way that only comes from the quiet partnership of survival— he, underground, and I, above, making sure it warmed our family. As we all sat around the table, eating our modest dinner, I noticed the familiar furrow of worry in my father's brow. He'd been quiet the whole evening, more so than usual. Suddenly, he set his fork down and looked straight at me, his deep-set eyes weary but determined. "Sean," he began his voice low but steady, "you've reached the age where

*From Hippie to Preacher*

you can legally leave school. You know we don't have much money, son. Think about it and let me know by tomorrow evening." His words hit me like a wave. I stared down at my plate, suddenly feeling like I was eating stones, not stew. The thought of leaving school had never crossed my mind. Sure, we didn't have much, but I'd always hoped I'd be able to finish at least. Now, the future felt like it was collapsing in on me. What was I supposed to do? Where would I even go?

That night, after me and my younger brother, Paul had washed the dishes, I trudged to our room. The three of us boys shared a cramped space, with two small beds pushed against the walls and barely enough room to move between them. Our three sisters had the same setup across the hall, while Mom and Dad had their own corner of the house, though even

that felt too small for the burden they carried. As I lay on the thin mattress, staring up at the ceiling, my mind raced. I could hear the faint sound of my brothers" soft breathing as they fell asleep, but sleep was the last thing on my mind. The idea of leaving school twisted in my head like a knot. How could I?

Where would I go? I didn't know the first thing about work, not real work anyway. The only thing I could think of was the mines— dark, deep, and endless. They'd swallowed up plenty of boys my age. Was that what awaited me? Eventually, exhaustion took over. I drifted into a restless sleep, but even in my dreams, the weight of my father's words haunted me. I found myself standing at the edge of a gaping black hole, the kind that led deep into the earth. Chains snaked around my wrists and ankles, pulling tighter with every

*From Hippie to Preacher*

breath I took. Suddenly, I was thrown into the mine shaft, plunging into the darkness, the cold, hard walls rushing past me as I fell deeper and deeper, until there was nothing left but silence and blackness. I jolted awake, my heart pounding, sweat clinging to my skin. The room was still dark, the sounds of my brothers' steady breathing the only thing grounding me in reality. But the fear lingered. It wasn't just a dream. It was a warning, a glimpse into what my future could become.
Tomorrow evening was coming fast. And I had no idea what to tell my father. That day at school, I found myself asking the boys in my class what kind of jobs might be waiting for me if I left. I wasn't sure what the future held, but I knew one thing: school was over for me..

*From Hippie to Preacher*

"You can become a fireman," one of them said, his voice full of the kind of certainty only kids seem to have. "Yeah, or the railways," another chimed in. "My brother left last year and works there now. He's real happy." He nodded like he was already picturing himself in his brother's shoes. "What about the mines?" a third suggested, his voice a little quieter, like he knew it wasn't the most exciting option, but it was there, always there. "The mine's always hiring." I nodded along, but none of it seemed to stick. Except for the fireman job.

After school, we piled onto the old bus that would take us back to our little mining village. The air was heavy that afternoon, thick with the kind of humidity that makes everything feel slower. As we rattled down the dirt road, the sound of thunder rumbled in the distance,

*From Hippie to Preacher*

low and steady like a warning. Everyone scrambled to the windows, pressing their faces against the glass. I glanced up just in time to see a group of bikers roaring past us. There must've been ten of them, maybe more, their engines growling like thunder of their own. They were nothing like what I'd seen before. They weren't rough, like the men from the mines or stiff like the workers in their uniforms.

They were free. They raised their hands as they passed us, flashing peace signs with easy grins on their faces. They wore floral shirts, loose and flowing, bell-bottom jeans that flared out like they had all the time in the world. The bus rocked as they sped past, and the others on the bus let out little gasps and giggles, talking about how strange they looked. But me? I couldn't look away. Deep in my chest, something stirred. It was like a door had cracked open, just a little, enough to let in

*From Hippie to Preacher*

the idea that there was more to life than the choices everyone talked about. Firemen, railways, the mines—they all faded in the noise of those bikes roaring past. And just like that, I knew. I didn't know how or when, but I knew one thing for certain. One day, I was going to own a bike. And I was going to be free.

The table was set, and our six children sat in a familiar line, eyes bright but hungry, waiting for the same meal we had eaten for ten of the past thirty days. My mom, always with that gentle smile, stood by the stove dishing out "melk kos," a simple porridge that filled our bellies though it never quite filled our hearts. I never liked it much. None of us really did. But it did the job. My mom's ladle moved swiftly, scooping portions into chipped bowls, the warm scent of cinnamon filling the small

kitchen. It made the house feel a little more like home, even on days when there wasn't much else to hold onto. My dad entered from the bathroom, wiping his hands on the frayed towel slung over his shoulder. His boots thudded against the worn wooden floor as he took his seat at the head of the table. We all lowered our heads as he gave thanks, his voice deep and steady. The meal began quietly, the younger ones slurping the warm melk Kos from their spoons, the sound somehow comforting in the stillness of the evening. My parents made small talk, mostly about the weather and the work in the mines, until my dad turned his eyes to me. "Have you given it any thought?" he asked, his voice carrying more weight than the words themselves. I swallowed, my heart beating a little faster. "Yes, Dad," I said, trying to steady my voice. "I want to become a fireman."

*From Hippie to Preacher*

The room seemed to freeze. My younger siblings stopped eating, wide-eyed and curious. My mom, her back to me as she wiped the counter, paused for just a second, her hand still. Everyone looked at me like I had just spoken some forbidden word. "A fireman?" my dad repeated, his voice laced with disbelief. He leaned back in his chair, crossing his arms. "That's not a job for a man, son. I see them all the time, coming to work in the mines. The money a fireman makes... it's nothing compared to a miner's wage."

I looked down at my bowl, the sweet smell of cinnamon suddenly sickening. "But, Dad, I don't want to be a miner," I said quietly. The room grew colder, and the tension between us felt like a heavy stone in my chest. "No," my dad said firmly, cutting off any further protest. "I'm bringing papers home tomorrow from

work. The mine's looking for apprentice boilermakers. That's what you're going to do. Boilermakers earn good money." And just like that, my future was sealed. My dream, a flicker of hope, had been snuffed out before it even had the chance to catch

The next day was Friday, a day bathed in warm sunshine as I walked to the bus stop. My thoughts drifted back to the boilermaker thing—what was it exactly? I couldn't picture what a boiler even looked like; let alone what a boilermaker did. How does one even make a boiler? The questions spun in my head, creating a knot of uncertainty. Paul, my younger brother, broke the silence, his voice casual yet reassuring. "Don't worry, Sean. Think of it this way—you'll earn money, and then you can buy that motorbike you're always talking about."

*From Hippie to Preacher*

I smiled a little at the thought, though the idea of becoming a boilermaker still weighed heavily on me. As the bus screeched to a halt at school, I spotted one of our classmates, Rudolf, standing nearby. I seized the moment and asked him, "Hey, do you know what a boilermaker is?" He shrugged a clueless expression on his face as he shook his head. "No idea. Why do you ask?" I explained, "My dad's bringing home some papers tonight for an apprentice position at the mine. They're looking for trainee boilermakers."
Rudolf's eyes lit up with interest. "Really? That sounds cool. I'll go with you, then. I'm not planning on sticking around for school next year either." He paused, a grin creeping across his face, the kind that suggested he had just stumbled onto something big. "Can you believe it? Only three weeks left of school for

*From Hippie to Preacher*

the year!" As we walked into the classroom, Rudolf nudged me. "Hey, do me a favour— ask your dad to bring an extra set of papers. I'll grab them from you on Monday." I nodded, feeling a wave of relief wash over me. Knowing someone else was thinking about becoming an apprentice too made the whole thing seem less daunting. And just like that, Friday didn't feel so heavy anymore. In fact, it was shaping up to be a pretty good day.

Eventually, the day arrived. My father dropped me off at the gates of the mine workshops. I glanced back to wave him off, then turned to see a group of young men standing nearby, many of whom I recognized from school. It was strange to see us all here— no longer students, but now something else entirely. Just then, I heard my name being called from across the road.

*From Hippie to Preacher*

"Sean!" a familiar voice shouted. It was Rudolf. He waved enthusiastically and then broke into a run as soon as the car that had dropped him off sped away. By the time he reached me, we were grinning like idiots, as if the world had arranged this moment for us to become best mates. We fell into conversation immediately, laughing and chatting as though we'd known each other for years, even though we hadn't been particularly close before. There was something about this place—about this day— that seemed to bond us.

A few of the boys who used to sneak cigarettes behind the school stood openly smoking now, puffing away like it was nothing. They were trying hard to look like grown men, and I suppose in a way, we all were. Most of us were just sixteen, but being

*From Hippie to Preacher*

here made everything feel different like a new chapter had begun.
Suddenly, the air around us shifted. A silence fell over the group as an older man approached, clutching a piece of paper in one hand. His presence demanded attention. He stopped a few feet in front of us and looked us over, his gaze hard and calculating.
"When I call out your name," he began, his voice gruff, "stand over there." He began reading from the list, one name after another. All eight of us were there, except for two who hadn"t shown up yet. After the roll call, he nodded and gestured with a thumb over his shoulder. "Come on; let's go to the mine store." We followed him across the yard, and inside the store, he handed each of us our new gear—overalls, safety boots, and hard hats. I remember the weight of the boots in my

*From Hippie to Preacher*

hands, the thick rubber soles that would soon be caked in dust and grime. With our arms full of equipment, we walked back toward the front of the workshop. The old man stopped us just outside the large metal doors. "Stand here and look inside," he said, his voice barely audible over the noise coming from within. The sounds were deafening. Metal clanging, engines roaring, voices yelling over the cacophony. Tomorrow, it would be us in there, part of the grind, the sweat, the dirt.

"Tomorrow, seven o'clock sharp," the man shouted, turning his back to us as he pointed toward a small office across the yard. "Dressed in your overalls, boots, and hard hats. You'll report to that office over there." We learned that it was the paymaster's office, where we would give our full names and IDs, and where every Friday—except this one,

*From Hippie to Preacher*

because we hadn't worked a full week—we would collect our pay at two o'clock sharp. Work hours would be from seven in the morning to four in the afternoon, with Saturdays going until noon. "Go home now," the man added, turning away from us. "Remember, you start tomorrow. Seven sharp."
As we began to disperse, I glanced over at Rudolf. We were both wearing the same uneasy grin, realizing that life had just taken a turn. Tomorrow would be the real beginning. The workshop, the paymaster, the long hours—it all seemed so much bigger than us. And yet, there we were, standing on the edge of it all, waiting to see what would come next. The wind tugged at my hair, blowing it into my face as I stood at the edge of the road, waiting to collect my annual leave pay. It

*From Hippie to Preacher*

whipped a few stray papers across the street, and I brushed the strands from my eyes, feeling their length reach my shoulders now— a sign of how much time had passed.

It was impossible not to think back to that first day, when eight of us had stood in this very spot, fresh out of school, eyes wide with both excitement and nerves. We were apprentices then, green and eager, the future stretching out before us like an uncharted road. But now, the year had gone by so fast. A blur of days and nights, weeks turning into months, marked only by the routine of collecting my wages in a brown envelope every Friday. The hours worked were always scrawled hastily on the back of it, and I'd go through them like some accountant, counting every minute, every rand. Half the money I handed over to my mom for boarding, like clockwork.

*From Hippie to Preacher*

It was only fair. The rest I split in half again, slipping it quietly into my post office savings account, my eyes on a bigger prize—a deposit for a motorbike. Not just any motorbike, though. A Suzuki 750 GT. I'd been eyeing it for weeks, staring through the showroom window every Friday after I picked up my pay. It gleamed under the lights, sleek and powerful, like it was just waiting for me to take it away. Today was different, though. Today, I'd finally saved enough, with my leave pay in hand to close the gap. Tonight, I would ask Dad to come with me, to sign on my behalf, because I wasn't 21 yet. I could feel the excitement buzzing in my veins, the anticipation of seeing my name on that ownership form. I could already imagine pulling into work after my leave, the envy of the other apprentices clear in their eyes as they watched me roll up on that gleaming Suzuki.

*From Hippie to Preacher*

The year had gone by so quick, too quick, but for the first time, I was ready for what came next. The wind had been relentless all day, howling through the mining village as I stepped off the bus from town. One thing about living here was that the bus service was reliable—every hour on the dot, from 5 a.m. to 6 p.m., you could catch a ride to and from town. No delays, no drama. That steady, comforting routine was one of the few things you could count on. But today, as the sun hung low on the horizon, casting long shadows over the dirt road, I was distracted. A parcel rested under my arm, crinkling with every step. Inside was my little spoil for the month—a brand-new floral shirt with a big peace sign on it and a pair of bell-bottoms. All bought with my hard-earned leave pay. Tomorrow, I'd be sporting them to fetch my new Suzuki. Just thinking about it made my pulse quicken.

*From Hippie to Preacher*

That evening, at home, the smell of mutton curry filled the small house—Dad's favourite. We gathered around the table, the warm aroma of spices mixing with the chatter of my family. Dad looked across at me, his eyes crinkling with pride as he said, "Well done, son. One year down as a boilermaker apprentice." I nodded, a little embarrassed but pleased. Everyone was happy tonight, a rare thing these days. I cleared my throat and looked at Dad, my voice just a little shaky with nerves. "Dad, uh... will you come with me tomorrow? To sign for the bike?" He paused, his fork hovering over his plate. "The Suzuki you"ve been going on about every night?" I grinned sheepishly. "Yeah. It's ready. The shop opens at 8 tomorrow since it's Saturday."Mom, always knowing how to smooth things over, chimed in. "Your dad will take you. Don't worry."

*From Hippie to Preacher*

Relief washed over me. I could already picture the shiny red machine, waiting for me at the dealership. I was smiling from ear to ear when the sound of a bike rumbled outside, cutting through the conversation. Fellies, right on time. Mom peered out the window. "He's early," she said with a chuckle.

Fellies, a fifth-year apprentice who rode a sleek 750cc Honda, had been a regular fixture in my life lately. He'd been teaching me how to handle big bikes—not for free, of course. There was always a beer or two in it for him. But it was worth every drop, as far as I was concerned. I stood up from the table, gave everyone the peace sign, and headed for the door. The evening was young, and we had plans. Tonight, like every weekend for the past six months, we were meeting up at Charlie's, the local roadhouse.

After that, the whole group would ride out to the club for a joll. With the wind still whipping through the trees and the night ahead full of possibilities, I felt ready for anything. The future stretched out like an open road, and I was more than eager to ride it.

The kettle sang softly atop the old black coal stove, its high-pitched whistle blending with the crackling of embers beneath. I placed the heavy bucket of coal down beside it, wiping the grit from my hands. Even though I had a million thoughts racing through my head this Saturday morning, it was still my job to keep the stove kindled, to make sure there was enough coal to last the day. But today was different. Today wasn"t like any other Saturday. Today was the day I was getting my bike. The thought of it sent a thrill through me.

*From Hippie to Preacher*

The beautiful red Suzuki 750 GT, gleaming under the lights in the bike shop showroom. I'd seen it every day for weeks, waiting for me like some kind of dream made real. And today, at last, it would be mine. I could already feel the weight of the handlebars in my grip, and hear the roar of the engine that would carry me out onto the open road.

The first light of dawn was just beginning to creep through the kitchen windows as I poured coffee into two chipped mugs, setting them out for Mom and Dad. Dad had the day off, a rarity, but that didn"t change the routine of my morning chores. I was startled by the sudden burst of energy as my brother Paul came bounding into the kitchen, grinning from ear to ear. "You're getting your bike today!" he said, almost bouncing on his toes. "Yeah," I replied, the grin spreading across my face.

"And I'll take you for a spin once I've got it."His eyes lit up at the idea, and without another word, he dashed down the hall to our sisters' room. "Sean's going to take me for a spin when he gets his bike!" I could hear his excited voice echoing through the house. I couldn't help but chuckle. I hadn't even gotten the bike yet, but the whole house was buzzing with the anticipation of it. It felt like the start of something bigger, something that had been brewing in the background of our lives. As the warmth of the stove spread through the small kitchen, I took a breath, letting the calm before the excitement settle in my chest. Today was the day, and I was ready for it.

As my dad pulled up in front of the bike shop, my heart started racing. My mom glanced over to the side and asked, "Aren't those your friends standing over there?"

*From Hippie to Preacher*

I grinned. "Yes," I said, feeling excitement buzzing in my chest. This Saturday was already shaping up to be the best one of my life. We stepped out of the car, a light morning breeze greeting us. I spotted Fellies and Rudolf near the gleaming Suzuki, their faces lit up like kids in a candy store. "What are you guys doing here?" I called out, striding over to greet them. "She looks groovy!" Fellies shouted, pointing at the bike like it was a treasure."Yeah!" Rudolf added, his eyes glued to the Suzuki as if it was the only thing that mattered. Just then, the shop owner walked over with a wide grin, looking like he'd just hit the jackpot. "Morning, sir, madam," he greeted my parents. My dad, always playful, asked with a chuckle, "So, where's that 50cc Sean wants to buy?" "750cc, not 50cc!" we all shouted in unison, bursting into laughter that echoed through the shop lot.

*From Hippie to Preacher*

"Shall we head inside?" the owner asked, motioning us toward the office. We followed him in, leaving Fellies and Rudolf behind, their hands still running over the curves of the Suzuki, inspecting every inch like it was already ours.

The office was exactly what you'd expect in a bike shop: old motorcycle tires stacked up behind the owner's desk, rims dangling from the ceiling, and posters of barely dressed women perched on sleek bikes lining the walls. On the desk sat an old oil tin, cut in half and repurposed as an ashtray. Everything smelled like grease and gasoline. The owner took a seat behind the desk, shuffling some papers in front of him. "Here are the documents," he said, sliding them toward my dad with the smoothness of someone who'd done this a thousand times before.

*From Hippie to Preacher*

My dad reached for the pen, but it was my mom who stole the moment. She opened her handbag, pulling out the deposit we had saved up, each bill crisp and carefully counted. She handed it over, and the owner scribbled out a receipt before standing up. He smiled again, his front tooth missing, but there was nothing but sincerity in his eyes. He reached out, shaking my hand with a firm grip. "Congratulations," he said, handing over the keys. I couldn"t get to the bike fast enough. As I approached, the owner called out, "I filled the tank for you!" His grin widened. "Enjoy it, kid."

I ran my hand over the cool metal of the Suzuki, my pulse quickening. This was it—the start of the best Saturday of my life. The red Suzuki 750 GT glistened in the midmorning sun as I pushed it out of the bike shop.

From Hippie to Preacher

The metal gleamed like a trophy freshly won. Rudolf and Fellies erupted in applause, their whistles cutting through the air like birdsong. Heads turned, and soon a curious crowd gathered, drawn by the commotion, swelling with each passing moment. Isn't it true, that crowds draw crowds? And on this particular Saturday, it seemed like the entire town had stopped what they were doing to come and see the spectacle — my new Suzuki. I stood there for a moment, letting it all sink in. The murmurs, the smiles, the nods of approval. There was magic in the air, something electric as if the bike had cast a spell over everyone who glanced its way. "She's a beauty, isn't she?" Rudolf beamed, clapping me on the back. His face was lit up with the same excitement coursing through me. Fellies, too, was grinning ear to ear.

*From Hippie to Preacher*

"Be blessed," my dad said softly from behind the crowd, his voice barely audible but filled with warmth that sank deep into my chest. I threw one leg over the bike, the seat fitting beneath me like it had been waiting for this very moment. Rudolf clambered on behind me, his laughter echoing in my ears. With a twist of the throttle, the Suzuki roared to life, purring beneath me as if eager to run. The crowd parted, whispers chasing us as we pulled away. And just like that, with the wind tugging at my hair and the open road stretching out before me, everything changed. In the blink of an eye, I had become something else. No longer just another face in the town, I was the rider of the red Suzuki, the one who slipped through life's routines like smoke on the wind. They started calling me the village free-riding hippie.

But it wasn't about the title. It was about the freedom that came with it. At that moment, I realized, I wasn't riding just to ride. I was riding to be alive. That Friday morning we were singing about peace and love, sitting on the hard tar, about fifty of us—hippies gathered together in a wide circle right in front of the entrance to the commando office in Oberholzer. The wind was wild, tugging at my long hair, sending it whipping across my face. The sun was high and unforgiving, casting its relentless brightness over us on that Friday morning. It felt like the whole town had shown up, standing in the distance, staring at us in a mixture of curiosity, suspicion, and confusion. The media had arrived too, photographers circling like vultures, snapping pictures with their bulky cameras. It was the time before cell phones and before TVs filled every home.

*From Hippie to Preacher*

As we sang, the sound of police sirens echoed far off, a distant whine growing louder with every breath we took. Soon, the wail was deafening, and with the screech of tires and the harshness of brakes, they arrived—police cars sliding to a stop, doors flying open. We held hands tighter, our voices swelling in defiance. Ferry sat in the centre, strumming his guitar with calm determination, his eyes closed as if the world around him didn't exist. We sang at the top of our lungs, our voices harmonizing and tangling in the wind: *All we want is peace!* Shouts of "Make love, not war!" rang out between the verses, echoing off the walls of the buildings. The tension in the air grew thicker, a low hum of unease, as the police began closing in. Their presence was heavy, but we didn't stop. The closer they came, the louder we sang: *All we want is peace!*

*From Hippie to Preacher*

Suddenly, they were upon us, pulling at us, trying to break the circle, their hands rough and impatient. The more they pushed, the more we resisted, our voices climbing higher, our fingers locking tighter. A cop grabbed me by my hair, yanking me backwards with a force that made my scalp burn. My head snapped back, and I felt like he might tear my hair cleanout. "Take it easy!" I shouted, my voice cracking, "Make love, not war!"

But they weren't listening anymore. They were ripping Ferry's guitar out of his hands, breaking it across their knees, smashing it like it was nothing. The aggression in the air turned palpable, and before long, the crowd began to scatter. Some of us left voluntarily, others dragged away, but the fight drained out of us under the weight of their boots and batons. I stumbled to my bike and swing my

leg over my throat raw from the singing and screaming, my head pounding where that cop had tried to rip my hair from my skull. My peace sign pendant felt heavy against my chest as I rode home, my body aching.

Paul, my younger brother, was sitting on the porch when I rolled in. "You're back early," he said, a curious look in his eyes as he stood up. "Yeah," I muttered, the exhaustion settling deep in my bones. I parked my bike next to the wall, running a hand through my tangled hair. "If you bring in the coal and chop some wood for the stove, I'll give you a ride on my bike later," I added, trying to muster a grin. With a mischievous grin of his own, Paul sprinted off to do his chores, eager for that promised ride. I dragged myself inside, collapsing onto my bed, the day's chaos still ringing in my ears. My head throbbed with the memory of rough

*From Hippie to Preacher*

hands and shattered guitar strings, and my throat burned with the echoes of the words we had shouted so passionately: *All we want is peace*.

"Sean!" My dad's voice thundered from the lounge, sharp and booming, sending our dogs scrambling under the bed. Even though I was half-asleep, his tone jolted me awake. I had just stumbled into bed a few hours ago, after a wild night out, and the last thing I needed was this. But when Dad yelled like that, it wasn't something you could ignore. Everyone in the house was already wide-eyed, staring at me as if I were about to walk into my own execution. Groggy, I dragged myself out of bed, my body still aching from lack of sleep. As I stepped out of the room, my siblings trailed behind, curious to see what kind of storm was about to hit.

*From Hippie to Preacher*

"Morning, Dad," I muttered, trying to ease whatever tension was brewing. He didn't even acknowledge my greeting. Instead, he slammed the front page of the Sunday paper onto the table with a backhand so forceful that the paper fluttered a little before lying flat. "Look here!" I picked it up, still rubbing the sleep from my eyes. And then I froze. My jaw literally dropped. There I was—on the front page of the newspaper, being dragged by my hair, in full view of the world. For a second, I couldn't breathe. Shock gripped me, and my mind raced to make sense of it.

"What happened?" Dad's voice so loud the neighbours probably heard. His face was red, veins bulging from his neck. "What in the world were you thinking? What will people at the mine say? What are the people in the village going to say?!"

*From Hippie to Preacher*

I opened my mouth to explain, to try and salvage the situation, but before I could get a word out, he cut me off. "What will my boss, the mine captain, think of this mess?" His voice climbed higher with each question as if he were building his own mountain of fury. "And the headline!" He jabbed a finger at the paper. "Read it out loud!" I glanced at the bold letters: **"Hippies Wreak Havoc in Town— Why Weren"t They Arrested?"** My heart sank even deeper. Dad shook his head, disgusted. "Why weren't you thrown in jail? That's what they're asking!" My mom had entered by this point, standing in the doorway with her arms crossed, a stern look on her face. "What will people think of us now?" she said quietly, but her words hit just as hard. "They'll think we raised you wrong. That we didn't teach you any discipline."

*From Hippie to Preacher*

Her disappointment cut deeper than Dad's rage. I couldn't stand there any longer, being chewed up by their anger, their fear of what others might say. Without a word, I turned and walked out, needing to escape before I exploded. I headed straight for the woodpile to chop wood for the stove, something— anything—to work out the frustration boiling inside me.

As the axe bit into the logs, my mind raced. I couldn't believe the paper. Are Hippies wreaking havoc? Sowing disorder? It was absurd. We were singing about peace, for crying out loud.

No one was causing trouble. But none of that was in the article. No mention of the music, the message, and the hope we tried to share. Just chaos and blame."Disgusting," I muttered to myself, throwing another log onto the chopping block.

*From Hippie to Preacher*

"We were there for peace, and they've twisted it into something ugly." The final blow in the article—comments from random bystanders. **"These useless hippies should be run out of town."**

The familiar hum of Suzy, my lovely Suzuki, echoed down the tar road as I approached the mine's workshop. The rising sun crept over the horizon, casting long shadows from the massive mine heaps, and I felt the cool morning air tug at my jacket. I pulled into the small patch designated for motorbikes, the routine of it comforting after my annual leave. It was Monday; the start of a new week, but this one had a strange edge to it. My first day back after some time away, and something felt off. No sooner had I turned off Suzy's engine than I heard a familiar voice, loud and boisterous, calling out from the distance.

Rudolf, is always the first to spot me. His lanky frame sprinted towards me, the same exaggerated grin plastered across his face. His eyes danced with mischief. "What did you guys get up to on Friday? I saw you lot on the front page of the *Sunday paper*!" He slapped his knee, doubling over in laughter. "And look at you —still got hair on your head, eh? Come on, spill it! What happened?" I gave him a half-smile, brushing off his enthusiasm. "Later, man," I said as I locked up Suzy. There was too much on my mind to entertain his questions now. Rudolf, as persistent as ever, fell into step beside me. "You won't believe what happened while you were away. We were working, right? Usual stuff, when out of nowhere, these army MPs stormed in and arrested Jakes!" His voice dropped conspiratorially as if revealing some dark secret.

"Jakes? Why?" I asked, raising an eyebrow. "Draft dodger!" Rudolf said with a flourish, clearly enjoying the drama of it. "He ignored his call-up papers, been drafted two months ago but never told anyone. They dragged him out like a criminal." I let out a low whistle. "Two months? He kept that quiet." Rudolf nodded vigorously. "You'd better watch out, Sean. You'll be next!" "I haven't received any call-up papers," I said, though I could feel a flicker of unease crawl up my spine. "No, not that," Rudolf said with a grin that told me he was about to stir up trouble. "The police! They're coming for you after Friday's little... adventure." I rolled my eyes, clicking my tongue in disbelief. "Nice try." Ignoring his dramatic predictions, I headed into the workshop. The familiar smell of grease, iron, and sweat hit me instantly.

*From Hippie to Preacher*

As I put my bag in my locker, one of the journeymen nudged me and pointed toward the foreman's office. "Louis is looking for you. "That was never a good sign. I exhaled, mentally preparing myself for whatever was waiting behind that office door. When I entered, I was met with the sight of Uncle Louis, the grizzled old foreman, sitting at his desk, a look of grim amusement on his face. A few of the older journeymen stood around him, arms crossed, and as soon as I stepped in, the room fell silent. The men gave me a once-over, shook their heads, and quietly filed out. "What have we here?" Uncle Louis said his voice gravelly but with that familiar twinkle in his eye. "Morning, Uncle," I greeted, trying to keep my voice steady. He gestured for me to sit, leaning back in his chair. "I saw you've been making headlines."

I shifted uncomfortably. "It wasn't meant to be anything serious. Just a bit of singing about peace." He sighed, rubbing the bridge of his nose. "Look, Sean. I don't care what you get up to on your own time, but you've got to be careful. These protests—if you want to keep working here steer clear of them." His eyes locked onto mine, his tone more serious than I'd ever heard it. "This is no joke. You don't want the wrong people asking questions. "I nodded, the weight of his words settling over me. Uncle Louis wasn"t the kind of man to hand out warnings lightly. "Understood. "Good," he said, his tone lightening a fraction. "Now get back to work before I have to draft you for something else. "With that, I left his office, feeling the weight of the world settle back on my shoulders. There were some things in life you couldn't just ride away from—not even on Suzy.

*From Hippie to Preacher*

Riding home from my first day back at work after my annual leave, I was filthy—covered in black soot and fine metal shavings. The bike roared under me, its familiar hum comforting after a long day. As I pulled up to the house, I could see Mom peering through the kitchen window, her face soft and warm, though I knew she'd have a few things to say about my state. Before I could even kick down the stand, Tony came charging out of the house, all smiles. Our youngest had a grin that stretched from ear to ear. "Hey, Sean!" he called, practically bouncing on his toes. Tony had always shared my love for motorbikes; his eyes constantly trailing after them like they were magic. I reached out and ruffled his hair, now slick with sweat and dust. "Hey, kiddo," I said, watching as he eagerly grabbed my work bag from the bike, his small hands struggling a bit with the weight.

*From Hippie to Preacher*

"You always give Paul a lift on your bike," Tony said, his voice bubbling with excitement. "When's it my turn?" "Soon," I chuckled. "One of these days, you'll get your chance."

Mom stepped out onto the porch just as I reached the door. "Hello, Sean," she greeted me with a smile that was warm, but laced with expectation. "How was your first day back at work? "Hi, Mom." I shrugged. "It doesn't even feel like I was gone." The scent of cinnamon floated through the open door, wrapping around me like a blanket. It could only mean one thing—melk kos. Mom"s specialty. "Go take a bath," she said, her voice a little firmer now. "And make sure you clean it, do it properly. Your dad will be home soon, and you know how he is about things being done right."

*From Hippie to Preacher*

I nodded, heading towards the back of the house where the old tub sat in the bathroom. We didn't have a shower—no one in our little mining village did. Bathing was a ritual here, and if you didn't scrub every inch, you'd hear about it later, when dinner was called, we all took our seats at the long wooden table. Dad sat at the head, as usual, his presence as solid as the old worn chair he sat on. I found my place opposite him, bracing myself for the usual rundown of the day. He looked at me, his eyes steady. "How was work? "Same old routine," I replied, keeping my voice even, though I knew where the conversation was headed. And then, like clockwork, he asked the question. "What did they say about you being on the front page? "I tensed slightly, trying to brush it off. "Not much," I said "Uncle Louis warned me to stay away from the riots." "We were sitting on the ground," I

countered, my voice low but firm. "Singing about peace and love. How is that a riot? "Dad's expression darkened. "It was a riot," he said sternly. "You were obstructing the personnel from entering the building. "And, "It was outside the Commando"s office," Dad replied sharply. "That's not something people forget. "Mom, ever the peacemaker, chimed in. "The neighbours asked if you were in jail."

I cringed. In our town, jail was a stain that bled onto the whole family. Once someone went to jail, the rest of us were treated like lepers. People cut ties, stopped talking, and eventually, the family moved away, starting over somewhere new where no one knew their past. Dad cleared his throat. "At work, everyone was asking me the same thing. "Paul, our middle brother, spoke up then. "At school, everyone thinks Sean's groovy."

*From Hippie to Preacher*

Dad shot him a sharp look, and Paul immediately fell silent. We ate the rest of our melk kos in a thick, uncomfortable quiet. The weight of the day hung over the room like the low-hanging mining dust that clung to everything in this village. I wonder when things had changed so much—when peace and love became something to be feared, and when my presence on the front page could turn our whole world upside down. Paul, the one who came right after me, had taken over the chore of kindling the fire. Every morning, he'd chop wood and haul in the heavy bucket of coal for the stove before heading off to school. That used to be my duty, but now, as a second-year apprentice boilermaker, I only stepped in when he was feeling too sick or worn out to manage. Life had a certain rhythm to it, a routine that never seemed to change. Work all week, then Fridays and Saturdays were for the

sessions—where we'd dance until the early hours of the morning, losing ourselves in the music, the sweat, and the freedom of it all. The sessions were always a spectacle. A live band would take the stage, the thrum of bass rattling through your chest like a heartbeat. The lead singer and guitarist, Ferry, was the real star. He was known as the best in the West, and when his fingers danced over those strings, you knew you were in for a night that could make the world outside disappear. And when we weren't at the sessions, there were the garage parties. Those were open to anyone and everyone—a wild, carefree mix of people, strangers and friends alike. That was life in our little mining village. We were what they called hippies back then. The community cast their sideways glances at our long hair, floral shirts, and peace signs dangling from leather straps around our necks. Bell-bottom jeans

*From Hippie to Preacher*

swayed as we walked, and our feet were almost always in those rough old sandals we called "Moses sandals." We flashed peace signs with our fingers, shouting our slogan to the world, *Make love, not war.* And in our own way, we believed in it—living day to day in that bubble of youthful freedom, thinking nothing could ever change us. For us, life was as simple as the rhythm of a song and just as fleeting. But back then, we didn't think about time. We were too busy dancing to care.

As I climbed off my bike, the familiar sound of Tony"s feet pounding the ground came closer. My little brother, always full of energy, was already running over, his face lit with excitement. "Sean, you got a letter!" he shouted, waving his arms wildly. "A letter? From who?" I asked, frowning. My mind raced. No one ever wrote to me.

*From Hippie to Preacher*

Tony shrugged, all innocent mischief, before reaching for my work bag. His fingers brushed over the seat of my Suzy, my Suzuki, and I could see the gleam of admiration in his eyes. He loved that bike, probably more than I did. "Mom's got it," he said quickly, already dashing toward the house like it was a race. As I made my way to the backdoor, my boots crunching over the gravel. I tried to think who could've sent me a letter. Maybe it was from work, though that seemed unlikely. I hadn't been in trouble or anything. Then, as I stepped inside, I saw Mom. She stood by the counter, rolling meatballs between her hands, her apron already dusted with flour. "Hello, Sean," she greeted me, her voice soft but warm, as always. "Hi, Mom," I replied quickly, my impatience growing. "Where's the letter?"

*From Hippie to Preacher*

She raised an eyebrow. "Who told you about the letter?" "Tony," I said, just as the little blur of my brother came bounding back into the kitchen, the letter clutched triumphantly in his hand. I took it from him and stared down at the envelope. It was brown, thick, and official-looking. A large, red stamp stretched across the front: **CONFIDENTIAL**. Mom stopped rolling the meatballs, a frown creasing her brow. "Open it, let's see," she said, her voice a little tight now. By then, all the kids had gathered around. Dot, the youngest, reached up on tiptoes to peer at the envelope. I could feel their curiosity pressing in on me as I carefully tore it open. I unfolded the letter and started to read aloud: "You are very fortunate to have been drafted to serve your country. The country needs men like you. You will report to the Artillery Corps in Potchefstroom on the specified date and time.

# From Hippie to Preacher

Failure to report will result in your arrest by the military police. "The kitchen seemed to be still, the words hanging heavy in the air. I quickly calculated the date. Three months from now. Three months, and I'd be leaving home, leaving my job, leaving… everything. Mom dropped the meatball she'd been rolling, the doughy sphere landing with a dull thud on the counter. Dot, with her ever-watchful eyes, quickly scooped it up and placed it back on the sink as if that would fix the moment.

I walked slowly to my bedroom, feeling the weight of the letter in my hands, the weight of my future suddenly shifted. Paul, my younger brother, followed close behind, always eager to offer something. "I'll look after your bike while you're in the army," he said, a grin spreading across his face. I managed a smile, though it didn't reach my eyes.

*From Hippie to Preacher*

That evening, the kitchen table was quieter than usual, except for the sound of forks clinking against plates of spaghetti and meatballs. Dad sat at the head of the table, eyes gleaming with a strange sort of pride. "The army's going to make a man out of you," he said, nodding as if the decision had already been made. I could see he was proud — proud that his son, the one that was called a useless hippie only a few months back, was on the front page of the Sunday paper. Is now heading off to serve the country. I knew he couldn't wait to share the news with his friends at the mine. But Mom? She hadn't said a word since I'd read the letter. She just sat there, quiet, lost in her own thoughts, her hands occasionally brushing her apron, as though wiping away something that wasn"t there.

*From Hippie to Preacher*

The younger kids were excited, bombarding me with questions. "Are you going to quit your job? Are you going to be a real soldier?" their voices overlapping. Beatrix, my eldest sister, looked across the table, her eyes sharp as she glared at Tony. "Yes, Sean is going to be a soldier," she snapped, silencing him. I could feel a storm brewing inside me, the weight of their expectations pressing down hard. But for now, I just sat there, staring at my plate, the taste of the meatballs suddenly bland in my mouth.
The next morning, I hardly notice the sky, heavy with clouds. My mind is occupied by a single thought—the call-up papers. Friday doesn't feel like a Friday, not anymore. My mom hands me the sandwiches she made for lunch, her face a little more solemn than usual. I greet her softly and step outside, making my

*From Hippie to Preacher*

way over to Suzy, my trusty bike. A pang of worry hits me as I wonder how I'll manage to keep her when I'm in the army. The engine hums gently beneath me as I ride to work, slower than usual. The familiar streets blur past, but the routine comforts me, grounding me in the moment, even as my thoughts spin elsewhere. When I get to the workshop, I head straight for the foreman's office. I knock twice, the sound hollow against the door. "Come in!" Uncle Louis's voice booms from inside. I step in, feeling the weight of the envelope in my hand. "Morning, Uncle Louis," I greet him, my voice steady. He glances at me, squinting slightly before nodding. "Morning." I open my bag, the zipper loud in the quiet office, and hand him the letter. His expression changes when he sees the official stamp. A smile tugs at his lips, but it's not a joyful one.

*From Hippie to Preacher*

More like a knowing smile, the kind someone wears when they've been down this road before. He opens the letter, reading it quickly, and then walks over to the large calendar on the wall. Without a word, he circles a date in red, the ink bright and final. He hands the papers back to me. "I don't want any MPs coming around here looking for you like they did with Jakes. You understand? "Yes, sir," I nod, tucking the letter into my bag again. Satisfied, he turns back to his desk, and I leave, the door closing behind me with a soft click. I barely make it to my locker before Rudolf appears his eyes wide with curiosity. "Why were you in the office?" he asks, barely able to contain himself. "I've been drafted," I say, my voice low. His jaw drops. "You got your call-up papers? I nod, already feeling the weight of the conversation settling over me like a heavy coat.

*From Hippie to Preacher*

Rudolf slaps me on the back, grinning now. "Where are you going?" "Artillery Corps in Potchefstroom." He whistles. "The folks behind us, their son went to the Artillery too. Tough lot." Then, after a pause, he adds with a grin, "You know, you could let me take the Suzuki off your hands. I'd keep it warm for you." I chuckle, shaking my head. "I'll think about it."

The rest of the day passes in a blur of metal and noise, but I work harder than usual, trying to push the thoughts of the army aside. The news spreads fast through the mining village, each person who hears adding their own comments, their own stories. By the time the sun sets, it seems like everyone knows. That night, at the session, I danced like nothing was waiting for me on the horizon. The music, the laughter, the lights—all of it feels distant but welcome.

*From Hippie to Preacher*

It"s an escape, however brief. For a few hours, I forget the call-up papers, the red circle on the calendar, and the looming days ahead. When I finally slip into bed, careful not to wake anyone in the house, the world is quiet again. The hum of the night fills the room, and as my eyes close, I know that tomorrow, the clouds will still be there. But so will I.

Saturday morning was draped in thick, heavy clouds, the scent of rain lingering in the breeze as I pulled up to work. My eyes stung from lack of sleep, but the thought of a short day helped. Saturdays meant we knocked off at 1 p.m. in the workshop, a small blessing in our week. As I stepped through the doors, I was surprised to see everyone turning toward me, greeting me with nods and muttered words. Even the journeymen, who rarely bothered to

acknowledge us apprentices, were giving me the same respect. The letter had come yesterday, the draft notice. And somehow, it changed everything. I never realized a single piece of paper could shift people's perception so much, but here I was, no longer just another apprentice but someone to be treated with a kind of reverence. The other apprentices, usually my equals, now regarded me with something that felt close to admiration. It was strange, this sudden transformation. Saturdays always carried a different mood in the workshop. Without the foreman breathing down our necks, the place felt almost relaxed. It was one of his perks — he didn't bother showing up on Saturdays, leaving us under Uncle Koos's watchful eye. Koos was the charge hand, and though he could be strict, he was easy on us apprentices, softer than most of the senior guys.

*From Hippie to Preacher*

As the hours crawled toward one, the rain finally came, starting as a light patter and then growing heavier. A few of the guys chuckled, making comments about how "this is why we drive cars," their eyes drifting toward me. But I wasn't worried. I had my leather jacket and my helmet, and my Suzy, my trusty Suzuki, wouldn't let me down — not even in the pouring rain. By the time I got home, though, I was soaked to the bone. The jacket had done little to keep the rain out, and I squelched through the house, dripping water all over the floor. Not even Tony, my little brother, came out to greet me. When I opened the back door, I found all my siblings staring at me, wide-eyed, taking in the sight of me standing there, drenched from head to toe. It was the kind of moment where you didn't need words. I just grinned, shrugged, and shut the door behind me.

*From Hippie to Preacher*

The time had passed too quickly, like sand slipping through my fingers. There was only this week left before I was due to report for duty at the artillery corps in Potchefstroom. It was a strange kind of limbo, knowing everything was about to change, but still holding on to the last moments of normality.

On Thursday, Uncle Louis—our foreman and a man who always seemed to have all the answers—walked with me to the paymaster's office. His heavy boots echoed off the concrete floors as we entered the dimly lit room. I held the call-up papers in my hand, the brown envelope at odds with the worn, oily grime of the workshop just behind us. Uncle Louis explained my situation to the paymaster, his voice steady and certain as if he'd done this a thousand times before. I handed over the papers, the final piece of proof that my life

was about to take a sharp turn. "Can everything be paid out this Friday? Including prorate leave?" Uncle Louis asked a firm request rather than a question. The paymaster, a middle-aged man with thinning hair and a perpetual squint, glanced over the papers and then nodded. "No problem." Relief washed over me. One more loose end is tied up. We left the office and walked back toward the workshop, where the familiar roar of machinery grew louder with each step. The noise was deafening, but soon it would be a memory, replaced by the sound of rifles and the thud of marching boots. Strange as it was, I wouldn't miss it. Though the work had been tough, the men had started to treat me with respect. And in a way, that camaraderie was something I'd come to appreciate. As we approached the workshop doors, Uncle Louis clapped a hand on my shoulder. "You can take Friday off after

*From Hippie to Preacher*

collecting your pay." "Thanks," I replied, though my thoughts were already racing ahead to what lay beyond. Rudolf, one of my friends, grinned as I passed by, slapping me on the back with a rough affection. He'd been acting as though my leaving was some great loss, constantly coming over to offer advice or tell me how much he'd miss me. It was hard to believe that, in just a few days, I'd be gone for a year. The week flew by in a blur of goodbyes, last-minute errands, and packing. By the time Friday evening rolled around, there was an air of anticipation at home. It was as if we all knew this was our last Friday together for a while, and it made everything feel heavier. Mom had gone all out, cooking dumplings with oxtail—my dad's favourite, and mine too. As we sat around the table, the warmth of the meal filled the room, but underneath it all was that quiet tension of

*From Hippie to Preacher*

unspoken things. Halfway through dinner, I turned to my dad. The clinking of utensils ceased, and all eyes turned to Dad as I asked about selling the Suzuki."
The room went still. For a moment, I regretted bringing it up. Then Dad nodded, slowly. "That's fine," he said quietly. It wasn't easy, selling the bike. It had been my pride and joy. But with army pay being less than what I'd made as a first-year apprentice, I couldn't keep up the payments. And besides, I wouldn't need it where I was going. Tony, my youngest brother, piped up, his eyes wide with concern. "Are you going to buy another bike when you come back?" I smiled at him, trying to ease his worry. "Of course I will. Don't you worry about that?" The conversation shifted to lighter topics—small talk, jokes, and banters. Then Paul, my younger brother, spoke up.

"Dad, can you bring me those apprenticeship papers next week? I'm turning sixteen, remember?" Mom jumped in, her tone stern but loving. "End of the year, Paul. Then you can leave school. "Dad smiled the kind of smile that meant he'd already made up his mind. "We'll talk about it. Maybe next year. "I grinned at Paul, teasing him. "Or you could just go to the army instead." He shook his head so vigorously that he started to stutter, which sent the whole table into laughter. It was the kind of laughter that held the sadness at bay, even if only for a moment. As the meal came to a close, I couldn't shake the feeling that this was it—the end of one chapter and the beginning of another. In a few days, I'd be off to the army, leaving behind the noise of the workshop, the comfort of home, and the familiar faces of my family. But for now, I let myself savour the warmth of the moment,

*From Hippie to Preacher*

knowing it would have to last me through the long year ahead. The sun hung low in the sky, a blazing reminder that it was already shaping up to be a scorching day. Not a single cloud to break the heat. My dad had taken a day's leave for Monday, clearing his schedule so he could drive me to Potchefstroom, where I had to report for duty at the Artillery Corps. I could feel the weight of the day in the quiet spaces between our small talk, a distraction to keep the anxiety from surfacing. "Did you pack everything from the list?" my mom asked a tinge of worry in her voice. "Yes, Mom," I assured her, trying to sound confident. "Don't worry, I've got everything."

The closer we got to Potchefstroom, the more the silence between us stretched, filled with unspoken thoughts and fears. My dad followed the signs marked **Army Base**, and as we

*From Hippie to Preacher*

approached the gate, it became clear we weren't alone. Cars were parked on the grassy verge beside the entrance, families gathered around, talking, laughing nervously—laughter that didn't quite reach their eyes. You could sense the tension, the nerves buzzing beneath the surface. Army personnel were weaving through the crowd, asking to see call-up papers. Beyond the gate, young men, much like me, stood in clusters, some already looking like they didn"t belong, others hardened with anticipation. We parked, stepping out of the car. Before I had a chance to catch my breath, an officer approached us. "Good morning," he greeted us, polite but firm. "May I see your call-up papers? "I handed them over, feeling my palms damp with sweat. He glanced at them and then nodded. "Ah, yes. You're with the Artillery. Head over to the group on the far left.

Behind the gate I'll give you five minutes to say your goodbyes." Five minutes. The weight of that time sank into my chest. Dad clapped a hand on my shoulder, his voice steady despite the emotion behind it. "Don't let the discipline break you. You can do this. You will do this. All the best." We hugged, his arms around me strong, but the moment was fleeting. Then came Mom. She stood close, her eyes wet, a single tear tracing down her cheek. We embraced, and she kissed my cheek, trying her best to hold back the flood of emotions threatening to spill over. I could feel her trembling as I pulled away. "I'll be fine," I murmured, though I wasn't sure who I was trying to convince. I slung my bag over my shoulder and walked toward the group, casting one last glance over my shoulder.

*From Hippie to Preacher*

They were still standing there, watching me, just like all the other families. I lifted a hand, waving to them one final time. Then it came— a rumble like distant thunder. The army trucks arrived, one for each group. And suddenly, the air was thick with shouting and orders being barked. In the chaos, we scrambled onto the trucks. My truck was headed for the Artillery Corps; the one next to us for the infantry. The roar of engines and voices filled my ears, and with that, we were off. As we pulled away from the gate, I watched the world I knew grow smaller in the distance, swallowed by the dust kicked up from the road. And so, I began a new chapter in my life.

The three months of basic training passed by in a blur. It felt as if time had warped, every day blending into the next, each one marked by the same relentless rhythm. It all began

*From Hippie to Preacher*

with that first day—hair shorn close to the scalp, the cold buzz of the clippers ringing in my ears, and the clinical smell of antiseptic in the air as we shuffled through medical examinations. By the end of it, we were kitted out in uniforms that felt stiff and unfamiliar, rifles heavy in our hands, and the reality of what lay ahead sinking in. From then on, the routine took over, driving everything else out of our minds. Five o'clock in the morning, without fail, we were jolted awake for PT. Our bodies were still trying to shake off the fog of sleep as we ran, muscles aching, the air cool against our skin, yet we pushed through. A quick shower followed, then breakfast in the mess—meals eaten in a haze, more a necessity than a pleasure. After breakfast, the drilling began. Hours on the parade ground, the sun climbing higher as we practiced formation after formation, our boots scuffs the dust as we

moved in unison, arms snapping to attention. By lunch, we were already drained, but the day was far from over. The afternoons were reserved for the shooting range. With full packs strapped to our backs, we ran—no, we slogged —our way there. The rifles we had awkwardly held on that first day now began to feel like an extension of our arms. We learned the art of precision, the sharp crack of gunfire echoing in our ears as we lined up targets and pulled the trigger. At four o'clock, it was the same brutal march back to camp, exhaustion clinging to us like a second skin. After dinner, we filed into the classroom, where our tired minds were expected to absorb navigation lessons, our eyes heavy, yet too alert to miss a single instruction. And this day after day, week after week, became our life.

*From Hippie to Preacher*

Saturdays were no relief. Instead of the comfort of camp, we were dropped far out into the veld, unfamiliar terrain stretching endlessly before us. There, we embarked on route marches, navigating the wilderness with nothing but our maps and compasses, the land our classroom, the night our blanket. The evenings were spent under the stars, the cool veld air biting at our faces. "I rubbed the grit from my eyes, my body screaming for more sleep." Sundays, they'd pick us up—army Bedford's rumbling across the veld to haul us back to camp. But even then, there was no real rest. The day was spent washing clothes, scrubbing our barracks until they gleamed in preparation for Monday's inspections. It didn't matter if the sun scorched our backs or if rain soaked us to the bone—there were no breaks. The relentless pace continued, unyielding, until finally, after three months, it came to an

*From Hippie to Preacher*

end. On that final Friday afternoon, we stood in full uniform, every crease sharp, boots polished to a high shine, rifles held with the ease of experience. The inspection felt like a formality by then, and when it was over, they told us what we had longed to hear: seven days" leave. A brief respite before the next phase of training, a taste of freedom before we were called back once more.

In those days, nobody thinks twice about picking up a hitchhiker, especially not a soldier. It was the '70s, a time when goodwill still roamed the roads freely. Folks weren't as fearful then, though maybe they should have been. Nowadays, it's too dangerous—a kind act too often repaid in tragedy. People get carjacked, worse, some lose their lives. But back then, if a troopie, as we were called, was standing along the road, you didn't wait long

before a car would pull over. Between Potchefstroom and the surrounding towns, it was practically a guarantee. Ketang and I stood there, boots heavy with dust, just off the shoulder of the road. We were fresh from base, trying to get home on leave, waiting for a lift like so many before us. A farmer's pick- up rumbled down the road and slowed as it neared us. He leaned out, his face half-hidden by the brim of a wide hat. "I'm heading to Fochville," he said with a nod, "where are you boys off to?" "Carletonville," Ketang replied, and I added, "Blyvoor. The farmer grunted, "Hop on the back. I'll get you as close as I can." We tossed our bags onto the truck bed and climbed up, settling in with the wind whipping at our faces. It felt like luck had smiled on us. The rumble of the engine and the rhythmic sway of the truck made the ride almost peaceful, even though my mind was

*From Hippie to Preacher*

already at home, imagining the familiar sights and smells. As we approached the turn-off to Blyvoor, the farmer glanced in his rear-view mirror, pulling over with a slow hiss of brakes. "This is where I leave you," he said, turning halfway to call out. "You'll be alright walking from here?" "Perfect, thanks a lot," I said, hopping off and grabbing my bag. I waved to Ketang as the truck pulled away, calling after him, "See you in seven days!" His reply was lost in the roar of the engine as they sped off, and I was left alone on the side of the road. The sun was just beginning to dip below the horizon, casting the sky in shades of orange and pink. It would be dark soon, and I wanted to get home before then. I started walking, the road stretching out before me. When another car passed by, its tires screeching to a sudden stop up ahead. I jogged toward it, and the driver leaned out, "Where you headed?"

*From Hippie to Preacher*

"East Dene," I replied, slinging my bag over my shoulder. "Hop in," he said. I climbed into the backseat, the weight of my bag heavy on my lap. "You're in the infantry, eh?" he asked, glancing at my uniform. "Artillery, Potch," I said, leaning back into the seat. "On a seven-day pass now. "Seven days of freedom," he whistled, shaking his head. "Then what? Off to the border?" "Don't know yet," I said, feeling the uncertainty settle in again. It was always looming, the possibility of being sent to the border. He dropped me off at the entrance to East Dene, just as the sky turned deep purple, the first stars peeking through the twilight. I thanked him, and he shook his head, smiling. "No, thank *you*— for keeping us safe." With that, he drove off, the car's taillights disappearing around the bend.

*From Hippie to Preacher*

Our house stood silhouetted against the fading light, smoke rising lazily from the chimney. The sight of it, with the smell of cinnamon in the air, filled me with a sudden rush of warmth and excitement. My legs quickened, and I ran the last stretch, stopping at the gate, out of breath but grinning like a fool. Dinner was melk kos tonight. I could already taste it. The gate squeaked as I pushed it open, a slow, deliberate action that quickly turned into a hurried walk towards the front door. My heart pounded harder with each step, the weight of time and distance between us urging me on. Reaching the door, I knocked—once, twice— then darted to the side, hiding in the shadows of the house. The door creaked open, and Paul stepped out, glancing around in confusion. His eyes darted past me before he spotted my silhouette. "Sean!" he screamed, a mixture of disbelief and joy in his voice. He ran towards

me, arms wide, pulling me into a tight embrace. "Hello, Paul," I greeted softly, trying to sound casual, though a lump had formed in my throat. His smile stretched from ear to ear, radiating pure happiness. We walked into the house together. The familiar scent of cinnamon filled the air, and the sounds of laughter and conversation echoed from the kitchen. As we entered, my boots thudded heavily against the wooden plank floors. When I appeared in the doorway, everything stopped. It was as if a ghost had walked into the room. For a brief moment, silence. Then the spell broke. Chairs scraped back, feet shuffled, and before I knew it, Tony, my youngest brother, was the first to wrap his arms around me, followed by the others. One by one, they greeted me, voices overlapping in excitement.

*From Hippie to Preacher*

Mom smiled, her eyes glistening with unshed tears as she reached for a bowl. "Sit down, Sean. I made our favourite—melk kos." Paul, who had taken my old spot at the table, quickly moved over without a word, offering me my seat back. I sat down, taking off my beret. As I placed it on the table, the room fell quiet again, their eyes lingering on my short hair and the uniform I hadn"t yet grown used to. And then, as if a dam had broken, the questions began. Everyone spoke at once, voices rising over the clinking of spoons and the slurping of the warm, creamy dish. Dad, who had been watching me quietly, finally asked, "How long are you home for?" "Seven days," I replied between bites, the simple words filled with more emotion than I intended. Mom looked at me, her face softening. "You've grown up so much, Sean. The army has changed you… turned you into a

*From Hippie to Preacher*

man." I smiled, but before I could say anything, Tony piped up. "How many terrorists have you shot?" I chuckled, shaking my head. "Not so fast, little man. I'm still at camp." His face fell slightly, disappointment clear in his wide eyes. After dinner, Dad motioned for me to join him in the lounge, and soon Mom, Dot, and Paul followed. The room filled with their presence, their quiet anticipation, as if they all needed to absorb the fact that I was really here. In the kitchen, my two middle sisters cleaned up, their laughter occasionally drifting in.

We talked, laughed, and teased each other in that way only families do. I could see the pride in Dad's eyes, and Mom's face was lit with pure happiness. I didn't know how much I had missed this until now.

*From Hippie to Preacher*

The evening seemed to fly by, with Beatrix eventually bringing in coffee. Tony, never one to miss a chance for mischief, grabbed my beret and marched down the hall, the oversized cap covering his eyes. The whole room erupted in laughter as he stumbled around like a little soldier. In that moment, surrounded by the people I loved, I realized just how much I had missed this place. No matter where I'd go or what I'd face, there was truly no place like home.

The bus hissed to a stop, brakes groaning as it settled on uneven ground. I stepped out, grateful that the service still ran between the mining village and town. It was one of the few things that hadn't fallen apart yet. Every hour, like clockwork, a bus came and went, tying the two places together like a frayed thread holding an old shirt.

*From Hippie to Preacher*

Across the road, two dogs snarled and fought a mess of teeth and fur, while their owners shouted uselessly. The wind, stubborn as ever, chased paper bags down the street, and the sun —well, the sun had decided it had better things to do, hiding behind a wall of grey clouds. I pulled in a deep breath, the smell of diesel and dust clinging to my lungs, and made my way toward the bike shop. A crowd of younger guys hovered around the entrance, all eyes fixed on the gleaming beauty on display: a Honda Goldwing 1000cc. The thing was a monster, all chrome and horsepower, shining like a star against the dull backdrop of town. I could feel the hunger in their eyes. Some of them might have even saved up just for a chance to dream about it. Inside, the owner, Norman, glanced up, his eyes sliding past me at first. I guess I didn't look like myself anymore—not with the buzzed hair and the

*From Hippie to Preacher*

army shave. But when I greeted him, recognition flickered. "Sean!" he barked, a wide grin spreading across his face as he slapped me on the back. "Didn't recognize you with that haircut. How's army life treating' ya?" "Seven days' leave," I muttered, shrugging, not in the mood to talk much about it. But Norman, always full of energy, didn't need an invitation to carry on."Ah, so they're sending you to the border soon, huh?" I just shrugged again, unsure myself, but the thought of it weighed on me. A revving engine outside cut through the noise in the shop. When I turned, I saw him—Fellies, his bike roaring like a wild animal. He parked with a reckless flair, swinging off the seat and catching sight of me. His face lit up like he'd won the lottery. "Sean! What the hell did you AWOL?" His voice carried, drawing looks from the others.

I laughed, shaking my head. "Nay, man. Just on leave." "Seven days? Perfect! I'll pick you up tonight. We've got a session to hit, man. You gotta come." "Yeah, sounds good," I agreed, not wanting to turn down a chance to get back into the groove of things. "How'd you get here?" "Bus," I said with a shrug. "I'll take you home later. No more buses for you!" Fellies grinned and tossed me a peace sign, the others mimicking him with their fingers in the air. Then his eyes fell on the Goldwing, and his grin turned manic. "Damn, look at this!" he shouted, circling the bike like a predator. He swung a leg over it, gave a sharp whistle, and ran his hands over the tank. "This is it. This is the one." A murmur rippled through the group as we all crowded around, the energy infectious. Fellies were always the one to stir things up, to make everything seem larger than life. He hopped off the bike, turned to

*From Hippie to Preacher*

Norman, and yelled, "We got to talk business, man!" Norman waved him into the back office, and we were left drooling over the Goldwing. It was the kind of bike you didn't just ride—you became part of it, the roar of the engine filling your veins. Minutes later, Fellies burst out of the office, the music on the shop's radio blaring, and shouted, "Friday! Keep it for me, Norman!" He slapped the tank of the Goldwing like it was a living, breathing thing, a wide grin plastered across his face. He kissed it, of all things, before swaggering past us like he already owned the world. We couldn't help but laugh, but inside, I knew that no matter what came next—whether it was the border, or the uncertainty of the next few days—there'd always be moments like this. Moments where the world felt just a little bigger, a little louder, and somehow, even in the chaos, a little more alive.

*From Hippie to Preacher*

The cottage pie tasted delicious. "Thank you, Mom," I said, and everyone around the table agreed, nodding and murmuring in approval. I glanced at Dad, a question forming in my mind. "Will you take me back to the army camp later?" He nodded, a simple gesture that felt heavy with meaning, and then Mom spoke up, her voice soft but reflective. "The seven days just flew by, didn't they?"
It was strange. In camp, seven days stretched like a lifetime, each hour weighted with duty and routine. But on leave, seven days felt like a whisper, barely there before they vanished. The contrast was unsettling, yet familiar, and something we all seemed to understand without needing to say it. Mom had a surprise for me. Her eyes twinkled as she put a small packet on the table. "I baked ginger biscuits, just for you to take back to camp," she said.

*From Hippie to Preacher*

The small talk continued, mostly about the army and the news Dad had read in the Sunday paper—updates on the war at the border, the usual talk that seemed far away yet always present. Then, as if to break the sombre mood, Mom placed a larger package in the middle of the table. Tony, my little brother, couldn't resist asking, "What's in there? "Mom grinned. "Donkey ears," she teased. We all burst into laughter, especially when Tony pulled a face, scrunching his nose and furrowing his brow. The laughter spread, filling the room, lightening the air. It was a much-needed break from the tension that always lingered when it was time for me to go back to camp. After lunch, Dad checked the time. "We'd better leave soon," he said, his voice calm but purposeful. "I don't want to drive back in the dark from Potchefstroom."

*From Hippie to Preacher*

I stood; knowing what was coming next, and went to change into my uniform. When I came back and, ready to leave, Mom appeared with her old Polaroid camera. She insisted on taking a few photos, the kind that printed instantly, the pictures pushing out of the back of the camera with that familiar mechanical whir. The photos always took a few minutes to develop, but there was something special about the anticipation. After the pictures, I said goodbye to my siblings. Paul, my youngest brother, was coming with us, so I didn't need to say goodbye to him just yet. But when I reached Mom, she hugged me tightly, her eyes glistening with unshed tears. I kissed her cheek, trying not to dwell on the sadness there."Goodbye, Mom," I whispered, and she nodded, her smile tight, her hand lingering on my arm.

The others shouted their goodbyes from the doorway as I climbed into the car. The drive back was peaceful, the road stretching out before us, dark clouds gathering in the distance. Dad filled the silence with news about the family, talking about how they might be moving to Welkom in the Free State. "They're looking for miners," he said, "and the housing there is supposed to be good."I nodded, though I could tell his mind was already made up. He'd go at the end of the month to check it out, but he reassured me not to worry. "We'll send you the new address, don't worry about that." As we approached the army gate, the weight of the moment returned. I grabbed my bag from the back seat and got out of the car. Dad and I exchanged a brief, firm handshake. "Take care of you," he said. "You too," I replied.

*From Hippie to Preacher*

I stood by the gate, watching the car until it disappeared around the corner. Then, turning on my heel, I walked through the gates, feeling the familiar sense of readiness settle over me once again. Whatever was waiting on the other side, I was prepared to face it. As the sun dipped beneath the horizon, one by one, the men began to trickle back into the barracks. It had been seven days of leave, a brief escape from the rigors of army life, and now, as each soldier arrived, we gathered in a loose circle, sharing stories of home. Laughter filled the air, a strange, warm contrast to the sterile, cold walls that had grown so familiar. There were tales of old friends, of lovers kissed goodbye, of families offering words of comfort they didn't believe themselves. Some arrived late, coming from far-flung corners, their faces etched with the fatigue of travel but still lit with the joy of reunion.

*From Hippie to Preacher*

By five o'clock that morning, the barracks stirred to life once more. Whistles pierced the dawn, sharp and unforgiving, pulling us back from the soft reverie of civilian life. Reality returned with a jolt—the army was relentless. The shouting started soon after, sergeants barking orders, dragging us out of our memories and into the present. It was time for PT, and they made us run. We ran until the sweat poured from us in rivers, the physical effort wringing every last drop of rest out of our muscles. The PT lasted longer than usual, the officers determined to remind us of the distance between the softness of home and the hardness of the barracks. Breakfast came and went in a haze of exhaustion. There was no time to savour it; there rarely was. By midmorning, we were ordered to the parade grounds. The sergeant major's voice, booming as ever, delivered the news: we were leaving

the camp. The plan was to head far out into the veld, into the wilderness. It would be rough, harder than we'd had it so far, and it would start immediately. Each of us was divided into groups of ten, and we were told to draw tents from the supply depot. Thirty minutes, they said. Thirty minutes to gather everything, clear out the barracks, and report to the vehicle park. The air filled with frantic energy, men rushing around in organized chaos, beds stripped, lockers emptied. Bedford's—those old, faithful trucks—were loaded, and we piled in, rattling off toward Bloubos, the place we would now call home. Bloubos was a far cry from the regimented life of the camp. No inspections here, no daily PT. But freedom wasn't on the menu either. Instead, we dug trenches, patrolled the dry land, set ambushes, and stood guard. Rain or shine, day or night, it didn't matter. The weekends were just as

*From Hippie to Preacher*

brutal as the weekdays, and it felt like they were trying to cram a lifetime's worth of training into us before we moved on to the next phase. Then came the gun drills. We worked with the G5 guns, a beast of a machine. Some people outside the military called it cannon, but to us, it was simply "the Gun." After all, we were artillery. It had a certain pride to it, knowing we were handling the same kind of weapon used in World War II, but it was also a sobering reminder of what lay ahead. Three months passed in that manner, the heat and pressure forging us into something harder, something sharper. And then came the orders: we were heading to the border. The camp in Bloubos buzzed with preparation, the tension palpable We received a final weekend pass before deployment, a chance to go home, to say our goodbyes. It was bittersweet. The excitement of leave

*From Hippie to Preacher*

clashed with the cold knowledge that, come Monday morning, we'd be on a plane to the Caprivi, the border, the unknown. Koos, a quiet but dependable guy from Welkom, offered me a ride. His brother was coming to fetch him, and I was grateful for the promise of a lift. I had my mother's address in my pocket, written in her careful handwriting and sent weeks before. The thought of home was comforting, but it couldn"t drown out the growing tension. We all felt it— the tightening in the gut, the whisper in the back of our minds. This weekend would be our last taste of normalcy. Monday loomed large, and with it, the flight to the border, to the Caprivi Strip, where the real test awaited. The sun hung low in the late afternoon sky, casting a golden hue over the quiet street as I stepped out of the car. Koos Shout 12 sharp Sunday as the car sped off.

*From Hippie to Preacher*

The warmth of the sun's last rays felt good on my skin as I took a deep breath, pulling out the crumpled address from my pocket, even though I had already memorized it. Welkom, in the Free State. Fairbairn 22. I was here. The street stretched out before me, longer and wider than the small mining village I'd grown up in. I glanced at the numbers on the gates as I walked, children on bicycles pausing to stare at me—this uniformed stranger in their midst. It felt strange, being back on familiar ground, yet not familiar at all. Every house I passed seemed to hold curious eyes, watching my slow progress down the street. Then, there it was—number 22, standing quietly behind a small front gate. My dad's old Ford Anglia sat parked under a grapevine in front of the garage, a testament to the life they had begun building here. I pushed open the gate, its squeak unfamiliar in this new place.

*From Hippie to Preacher*

Before I could take another step, my eldest sister, spotted me from where she was chatting with the neighbour's daughter at the fence. Sean! Her screams of delight pierced the quiet air as she came running toward me, arms open wide. We hugged tightly, the moment pulling us into a familiar embrace. The front door creaked open, and there stood my mother, tears of joy streaming down her face. I didn't even have time to greet her before she wrapped me in her arms, holding on as if she'd never let go. The younger kids swarmed us, all eager to say hello, to touch the brother they hadn't seen in what felt like forever. "Shh," Mom whispered after a while, wiping at her eyes. "Your dad is sleeping. "We moved into the kitchen, and I was struck by how different everything seemed. It wasn't just the house that was new—it was the feeling. The heart of the home, the kitchen, was

unrecognizable without the familiar coal stove I had grown up with. I stared at the electric stove, blinking in mild surprise. "This isn't the same," I muttered, unable to keep the disbelief from my voice. Mom smiled, nodding at the stove. "No more chopping wood or worrying about kindling the fire. Paul doesn't miss it, do you, Paul?" Paul, my younger brother, gave a small grin as he reached for the sugar bowl. "Not at all." He winked, "No more waking up early to make sure the fire doesn't go out. It's a good thing." We all chuckled softly as Mom poured coffee for everyone, and we settled around the kitchen table—just like old times. The conversation flowed easily, like slipping into a pair of worn-in boots. I asked if they were happy here in Welkom. "It's much bigger than Blyvoor," Mom said, nodding thoughtfully. "More shops, more places to go. It's growing on us. Beatrix, my eldest sister,

chimed in with a bright smile. "The school is lovely. I've already made lots of friends." Her excitement was palpable. The two youngest, Tony and Dot weren"t so convinced. "We don't like it," they grumbled, their little faces scrunched in discontent. "Why not?" I asked, trying to keep from laughing at their seriousness. "The school's too far to walk to!" Tony complained, crossing his arms in a huff.I couldn't help it—I laughed, the sound spilling out into the comfortable warmth of the kitchen. We kept chatting, small talk weaving through memories and new experiences. Dad was working shifts here, and apparently, he enjoyed it—more free time, more room. The house, they proudly told me, had four bedrooms. "Where do I sleep?" I asked, looking around the cosy but full kitchen. Mom"s smile widened. "Your dad converted the servant's room outside. You'll have your

*From Hippie to Preacher*

own space." "That's nice," I nodded, feeling a surprising sense of relief at the thought of a space just for me. Paul stood up, grabbing my bag. "Come on, I'll show you." I followed him outside, feeling a little lightheaded from all the warmth and welcome. The room was small but neat, and there, on a shelf Dad had built, was my record player. I placed my bag down, sitting on the bed as I took it all in. This was the first time in my life I'd have my own room. Not even in the army had I slept alone. I rifled through my small collection of records, fingers brushing over the familiar vinyl, before settling on a 45. I set it on the turntable, turned up the volume, and let the familiar strains of music fill the room. The song began, carrying me away with its words. "I wanna give you 40 days... to get back home..." And for the first time in a long while, it felt like I was home.

I had just changed into my civvies, my clothes hanging comfortably after the stiff uniform, and made my way to the kitchen. The air was warm, filled with the comforting smell of fried onions and mince sizzling in the pan. The homeliness of it all wrapped around me, soothing the nervous energy that had been building up inside. I took a seat at the kitchen table, watching Mom move about, busy as always, stirring the pot of pasta."Smells good, Mom," I said, trying to keep my voice casual. She glanced at me with a small smile, her hands never pausing their steady work. Just then, Dot, my youngest sister, came bounding in, her hair flying behind her. "Dad"s up. He wants tea."Mom, without missing a beat, set the kettle on the stove. The sound of water filling the teapot filled the room as she poured. A moment later, Dad walked in. His step was slower, but his eyes still carried that sharpness,

*From Hippie to Preacher*

the same look he always had when he was sizing something up. He looked at me and grinned. "Are you on AWOL?" he asked, teasing as always. I stood up and gave him a hug, the smell of gin and old leather clinging faintly to him. "No way, Dad. Not me." His smile deepened into something knowing. He'd been through it all himself. "I'm glad you got a weekend pass. Thought you'd come say goodbye before you head off to Caprivi." "Yeah," I said, trying to keep the mood light. "Wanted to see everyone before I leave. It is going to be anything from three to six months." Dad shook his head, leaning against the counter as Mom handed him his cup of tea. "Three to six months, huh? There are no tanks or guns up there. "No," I admitted, "it's all patrols and setting ambushes. We've been practicing that for months now."

He studied me for a moment, his eyes narrowing slightly. I knew he was worried. "After six months, you're done, right?" I nodded. "Six months, and I'm finished with it all." A pause, then he asked, quieter this time, "And after that?" I looked down at my hands. "I'm going to resign at Blyvoor. I'll finish my apprenticeship here in Welkom." He let out a long breath, his face softening with approval. "Good." He smiled at me, his face a little brighter. "I'll keep my ears open, see who is looking for apprentices." We finished our tea, and as the last of the light faded, we walked outside. The sun had dipped below the horizon, leaving the world in shadow, a kind of quiet settling over the neighbourhood. As we strolled toward the garage, he asked me something that had been hanging between us all night.

"Are you scared to go to the border?" I glanced at him, surprised by the directness. "No, Dad. It's going to be an adventure." I tried to sound convincing, but I wasn't sure if I was doing it for his sake or my own. "It's something I need to do. For the country. But I'm not staying in the Permanent Force. I'm just a draftee, and that's how I'll stay." Dad stopped in front of the garage door, resting his hand on the handle. "Just look after yourself," he said softly. There was no teasing in his voice now. I nodded. "We're a team of ten in our section. We've got each other's backs." Satisfied with that, he unlocked the garage and flicked on the light. The space was filled with tools and old odds and ends. A large wooden box sat against the far wall. He walked over, opened it, and rummaged inside. After a moment, he pulled out a dusty bottle of gin, the glass gleaming under the dim light.

# From Hippie to Preacher

"Dop?" he offered, already pouring some into a tumbler on the workbench. I shook my head with a grin. "No thanks, Dad." He downed the drink quickly and then wiped his mouth, stashing the bottle back in the box. "Don't tell your mom," he said, chuckling softly. I laughed, but something about the moment felt heavier than it should have. Maybe it was the weight of the upcoming months, the distance from home, from everything familiar. Or maybe it was just knowing that Dad, with all his quiet strength, was trying to say goodbye in his own way. "How do you like it here in Welkom?" I asked, changing the subject. He paused, looking out over the backyard where the last traces of light were fading. "Should've moved here years ago," he said his voice low. Before I could respond, Tony appeared at the door, his little face bright in the evening gloom. "Mom's calling! Food's ready!"

From Hippie to Preacher

We both turned back toward the house, the warm light spilling out from the kitchen. As we walked, I could hear Mom's voice from inside, talking to Dot, the clatter of plates being set out. The sound of home. For a moment, I let myself believe that everything would stay just like this. But deep down, I knew the world was already shifting under my feet. But as it is with everything else, time doesn't stand still. When I sat up, yawning and stretching my arms toward the ceiling, I noticed the sun was already streaming through the curtains. Today was Sunday—my last Sunday morning with my family. I peeked through the curtain"s gap, squinting into the stillness outside. The street lay quiet, unnervingly so, as if the world had paused. After staring out for a moment longer, I shrugged it off, letting the thought dissolve as I padded across the room into the small,

humble shower. I was glad to have my own space here, even if it was outside the main house. Privacy was a luxury, one I didn"t take for granted. After shaving and feeling the morning chill retreat from my skin, I ambled over to the turntable, carefully pulling out a worn 45 record. I set it spinning, and the familiar melody of *Baby Blue* floated through the air, weaving itself into the quiet of the morning. The song felt like a soundtrack to my thoughts—soft, nostalgic, a little sad, the days stretching longer than they should. A knock on the door broke the song's spell. "Come in," I called. The door creaked open, revealing my brother. "Hello, Sean," Paul said, stepping inside. "Hi, boet," I replied, smiling at him. "Everyone still sleeping? "No, they went to church". "Church?" I asked, confused. "Since when?"

"Since we moved in," Paul explained with a shrug. "Aunt Stena from next door invited Mom to go with her one Sunday, and now the whole family goes—Dad, too, when he's not working." I furrowed my brow, not fully processing this new tradition. "Where is this church?" Paul pointed out the door. "You can see the tower from the front gate. Come on, let me show you." I slipped on my sandals, and together we walked down the path. The front gate stood rusted but sturdy, a little portal to the outside world. Paul pointed down the road. "There, see?" In the distance, over the tops of trees, a steeple peeked out, proud and unwavering. I nodded, just as we saw a group of people walking toward us. I squinted, unsure for a moment. "Is that them?" I asked, glancing at Paul. "Yep," he confirmed. "They're finished."

From Hippie to Preacher

We stood together in the doorway, waiting for them, our family to come Six months, just six months left, and then I'd be done. Done with the service, done with the sand and the sweat, and the long days under the burning sun. It felt close enough to touch, that freedom. This thought reminded me—I needed to get dressed. Koos was picking me up at noon sharp, down at the corner. After we finished tea, I excused myself and went to my room. The uniform waited there for me, neatly folded, a symbol of duty, pride, and everything that came with it. I dressed quickly, not wanting to linger on the tightness in my chest, the subtle pull of homesickness that gnawed at the edges of my resolve. As I was adjusting my collar, Dad appeared in the doorway, his arms crossed, a familiar look on his face.

From Hippie to Preacher

"When are you guys leaving for the Caprivi?" he asked his voice even, but his eyes told me more. "Tuesday," I replied, meeting his gaze. "We're flying out from Bloemfontein. They said we could be there for anything from three to six months." I paused, letting that sink in. "We're getting danger pay though. Maybe I'll have enough to buy a bike again by the time I'm back." Dad just shook his head, a faint smile tugging at the corner of his lips. He knew how I'd been saving up, for that bike. He didn't need to say anything more. Mom bustled into the room, a cake tin in her hands. "Here, put this in your bag," she said, pressing it into my chest. "But don't open it now. Wait until you get to the camp." Then she handed me a smaller bundle, wrapped in a dishcloth. "This is for the car ride. You boys will need lunch." Her voice wobbled just slightly as she spoke, and I saw her blink away the tears

threatening to spill over. After all the hugs and farewells, after Mom shed her few tears, I turned to go, my bag slung over one shoulder. But then Paul, my younger brother, jogged up beside me. "I'll walk with you to the corner," he said, grinning, though there was seriousness in his eyes, the same look Dad had just given me. We talked and laughed as we strolled down the quiet street, making light of everything, but the weight of my departure hung in the air between us, unspoken but felt all the same. At the corner, a car pulled up with a squeak of brakes and a puff of dust. "Well, this is it," I said, offering Paul a quick, firm handshake. "Take care, Sean," he replied, his voice just a little softer.

I climbed into the car, tossing my bag into the back seat. Koos grinned at me from behind the wheel. "You ready?"

## From Hippie to Preacher

"Always," I said, though my stomach fluttered slightly. "I've got some lunch with me," I added, holding up the bundle from Mom. "Me too," Koos chuckled. "We'll stop at the Vaal River and eat." "Sounds great," I said, settling into the seat as the car rumbled to life and we set off toward Potchefstroom. The road stretched ahead, long and uncertain, but for now, we drove into the afternoon, laughing, the world shrinking to the two of us and the miles rolling beneath our tires. The road was surprisingly busy as we drove out of Welkom, heading towards Potchefstroom. Koos's brother had fetched us on Friday afternoon, but today Koos was driving himself, steady behind the wheel. His plan was to pick up his girlfriend's brother in Orkney, and then, once we reached Potchefstroom at the army camp, he'd keep the car with him until we returned from the Caprivi.

As we reached the Vaal River, Koos pulled the car over. We decided to enjoy our lunch by the water. My mom had packed us a little something, and we ate quietly, the roast chicken in the savouring peacefulness that the river offered. After spending a good while throwing stones into the shimmering water, watching the ripples spread, we got back into the car. Crossing the bridge, we entered the Transvaal. Orkney was just a short drive away, nestled by the riverbanks. Koos steered the car smoothly through the quiet streets until we reached his girlfriend's brother's house. Mike, a miner, was out front, watering his lawn with a hosepipe when we pulled up. He looked up and, with a broad grin, shouted, "Hey, Kosie!" Koos greeted him, introducing me as Mike shut off the tap.

From Hippie to Preacher

"Would you guys want something to drink or eat?" Mike asked, wiping his hands on his shorts. "Nah, we're good," Koos replied, shaking his head. "We better get moving to Potch. It's not too far." Mike disappeared inside the house for a moment to grab his flip- flops. He came back, hopping into the front seat next to Koos while I slid into the back. As we drove, Mike talked about life in Orkney, mostly about the mines and the housing shortage they were facing. The conversation drifted to cars, bikes, and, of course, girls. The drive passed quickly, and soon enough, the skyline of Potchefstroom appeared in front of us, the air warm and still on this beautiful Sunday afternoon. Koos pulled the car to a stop right in front of the army gates. We got out, grabbed our bags, and said our goodbyes.

From Hippie to Preacher

Mike blew the hooter, gave us a final wave, and sped off as Koos and I walked through the gates, ready for the next adventure. The regiment stood huddled just inside the gates of the army camp, the fading light of the sun replaced by the deep indigo of night. A cold breeze snaked through the air, raising goose bumps on my skin. One thing we'd all learned about the army was simple: *hurry up and wait*. The officers stood off to the side, clearly waiting on orders from somewhere higher up the chain, while the rest of us chatted in small groups, sharing stories about weekend leave. Laughter rang out here and there, cutting through the organized chaos, but beneath it all, a subtle nervous tension hummed. It was the kind of feeling that came before something big, but undefined.

## From Hippie to Preacher

We couldn't retreat to the barracks—other soldiers were already asleep in there, blissfully unaware of whatever was happening outside. Bloubos was out too; that row of tents we had pitched three months ago was full. The dew had started falling, soaking into our uniforms, and the chill in the air felt sharper by the minute. Suddenly, a voice cut through the murmur of conversation. "Fall in!" the sergeant barked, and just like that, the familiar routine snapped us to attention. We marched, the sound of boots on gravel in perfect unison, towards the vehicle park. Rows of Bedford's were waiting for us, hulking shadows in the dim light. We were loaded up quickly, the engine's rumble filling the night air as we jolted forward. I glanced at my watch—it was already 9 p.m. We were heading to Bloemfontein, deep in the Free State.

## From Hippie to Preacher

The convoy snaked through the darkness, headlights cutting brief tunnels of visibility into the night. Hours passed, the hum of the trucks becoming a steady, numbing rhythm. By the time we arrived at Tempe Military Airport, it was well past 1 a.m. The air felt colder here—much colder than Potchefstroom—and we were greeted by nothing but the biting wind. They gathered us near the stores, the dim glow of floodlights casting long shadows across the concrete. We were issued R1 rifles—*old school* but reliable. No one said much, but we all sensed it: something was happening, something they didn't want the outside world to see. There were whispers about spies, secrecy, and the importance of keeping this whole operation under wraps.

# From Hippie to Preacher

Rifles slung over our shoulders, webbing strapped tight, we marched once more, this time to a nearby hangar. Inside, the air was colder still, the metallic scent of the place mixing with the dampness on our skin. We settled in, back-to-back on the cold floor, trying to share warmth as best we could. The word passed around: we were waiting for the *Flossie*. That's what they called the plane. I"d never flown in a military transport before, and as we sat there, exhaustion weighing us down, thoughts of the coming flight mingled with the gnawing cold. One by one, we started to nod off, heads drooping onto shoulders. Bloemfontein, with its sharp winds and starless skies, lulled us into an uneasy sleep, though we all knew deep down it was just the calm before the storm. "Wake up! Wake up! Fall in! Fall in!" The calls tore through the hanger, jolting us upright where we sat, backs

leaning against each other on the cold concrete floor. Through groggy eyes and the haze of early morning, we could make out the faint silhouette of the "Flossie" on the tarmac—the old Hercules transport plane waiting to take us to the border. The Caprivi.

Slowly, we rose and lined up, shuffling into position, watching the "ou manne" descend from the aircraft. These were the veterans, just back from their tour, anywhere from three to six months on the front. It was barely four in the morning, and the hangar was still cloaked in a heavy darkness, the kind that made it feel as if dawn might never come. As the ou manne walked past, their eyes bore the weight of stories they would never tell. A few managed a smile, relief clear on their faces, savouring the knowledge that this was the end of their army life. But there were others, those

From Hippie to Preacher

whose gazes held something more permanent—men who, having tasted this life, would soon find themselves enlisted as permanent staff. For them, this wasn't an ending but the beginning of an unending tour. Finally, with the veterans safely on the ground, we began our march toward the plane, its hulking form almost camouflaged in the pre-dawn murk. Air force personnel bustled around the Flossie, refuelling and checking gauges, their shadowed figures moving swiftly and efficiently, their faces barely visible under the sparse lights. Everything had to be perfect. Once aboard, we settled into our places. The ramp groaned shut behind us, and the sounds from outside were swallowed up as the engines roared to life. A low, deep hum spread through the metal beast, the plane beginning its taxi down the runway. Exhausted, each of us surrendered to the engine's lull, leaning

back against the vibrating walls, eyes drifting shut. We'd be in the Caprivi in two and a half hours—a long enough journey to catch a few precious moments of sleep before whatever came next. The Flossie roared on, a fragile vessel carrying us closer to the unknown. The sun was already blazing down as the Flossie touched down on the scorched tarmac of the army airstrip. Heat waves shimmered off the runway, casting a mirage of water where none could be found. Just hours ago, we'd left the icy chill of Bloemfontein, and now, as the ramp lowered, the dry furnace of the Caprivi welcomed us with a gust of wind that hit like a wall. As we stepped onto the blistering ground, the reality of our new world set in. Our kit was unloaded swiftly, and then we were lined up and marched to the waiting trucks, sandbags stacked high along the sides our only protection if we hit a landmine. Each

## From Hippie to Preacher

of us carried our rifles with care, loading the magazines with deliberate hands before hoisting ourselves onto the trucks. We rumbled forward, the trucks moving cautiously along the notorious road known as the "Kaplyn." Dust churned up in white clouds that clung to our skin, a dry, relentless powder that would be our constant companion here. The Kaplyn itself stretched endlessly, a pale ribbon winding between the dense, thorny green of the bush. There were no sounds but the distant cry of birds and the hum of our convoy as we travelled, each of us staring out, Alert for movement in the thick brush on either side of the road. By afternoon, the sun high and unyielding, we arrived at camp in Ruakana, a bleak outpost surrounded by a perimeter of trenches and fortified bunkers.

From Hippie to Preacher

As we climbed down from the trucks, we were all blanketed in a thick layer of white dust, a uniform of sorts before we'd even unpacked. We were marched to the tents that would be our home for the next three to six months. They flapped weakly in the warm breeze, and after stowing our gear, we took some time to wash the dust from our faces and hands. Around us, soldiers in PT shorts and vests lounged or played volleyball, enjoying whatever brief reprieve they could find. Others lay on cots, absorbed in letters from home. The pace here was different, slower in some moments, but fraught with tension in others. That first night, we were briefed on our new routine. We'd be heading out on four-day patrols, lugging enough food, water, and ammunition to sustain us for the entire stretch.

# From Hippie to Preacher

Every patrol meant carrying supplies not only for ourselves but for the whole squad, everything we might need out there. When we returned to camp, we'd have two days to clean our gear, wash our clothes, and rest. Those days would be followed by duty "push beat"—guarding the bunkers that circled the camp. Four hours on, four hours off, an endless cycle of watchfulness and waiting. The ritual of "Klaarstaan" punctuated each dawn and dusk. Before the sun cracked the horizon and as it dipped each evening, the whistle would sound, and every soldier in camp would gather in the trenches, rifles in hand, eyes scanning the landscape for any threat. It was a time of heightened alert, our senses sharp, our bodies tense as we waited for the signal to relax. Patrols carried us far into the bush, marching under the blistering sun, through rainstorms, and even through the eerie stillness of night,

our destination an ambush point or some hidden hideaway. And so it went, day after day, the routines taking shape against the harsh, rugged beauty of the borderlands. It was a life lived on the edge, our world defined by sand, dust, and the weight of the gear on our backs. Yet, even in those moments of exhaustion and tension, something unspoken grew among us—a bond, forged under the relentless sun and the heavy silence of the bush, as we faced whatever came next, together. Out on patrol, life felt raw and stripped down to its core. No camp duties, no monotonous cleaning up, and no sandbags that seemed to grow heavier with each shovel of sand. Out here, we had just one job, and all the rough edges that came with it. Daytime meant dust and flies swarming relentlessly, sticking to our sweat-slicked faces, catching in every breath. Night-time was a different beast.

# From Hippie to Preacher

It wasn't just the enemy we kept an eye out for but the things that prowled unseen, the lions and the hyenas, both circling unseen, a constant reminder that we were part of their world. Our skin was always damp, drenched in sweat during the day, sometimes chilled by nightfall. And the scent of the bush—it's dry, earthy musk—clung to us, became us. We didn't just smell like the bush; we belonged to it, as much as the throne acacia and the dusty antelope tracks. Water was precious, carried in bottles as if it were treasure. When our rations ran low, we'd drink from muddy pools in the veld, knowing the choice was between the bitter tang of mud and the sharper pang of thirst. For six long months, the patrols became our life. Not all of us made it home. One of us was lost in an ambush, a reminder of the fragility of the quiet, uneasy peace that hung over our days. But the rest of us —well, we did

## From Hippie to Preacher

make it. Six months was all we had to give if we chose, or we could go the slower path, come back year after year. But who wanted to drag it out? We all chose to get it over with, to finish in six months. We were worn and weary, yes, but after that last patrol, we knew it was behind us, and we had the rare gift of walking away from it—homeward bound.

We were playing volleyball in the rough, dry air stealing the last remnants of energy from us. A few guys lounged nearby, reading letters from home, grinning at familiar handwriting or sighing at bittersweet news. Others sat cross-legged, chatting in soft, drifting tones that floated above the dirt in the fading light. Then, as if on cue, the rumble of engines sliced through the quiet, and we all turned to see the line of trucks rolling in. Our replacements had arrived.

# From Hippie to Preacher

They looked just like we had back then—worn out, tense, eyes wide against the blinding whiteness of the Kaplyn road, the thick, chalky dust coating their uniforms and faces like ghostly masks. They climbed down stiffly, blinking in the dim light, like they were surfacing from a long, strange dream. An officer barked orders, guiding them to their tents, pointing out where they'd sleep, where they'd wash the journey off their skin. We watched, a strange feeling brewing in us. Our bags were already packed, piled in heaps near the departure line, waiting with us for morning. Tomorrow, after "klaarstaan"—the last formal roll call—we'd load up into those same trucks, bound for the airport. "Flossie," the plane everyone looked forward to, would finally take us home.

# From Hippie to Preacher

The new ones seemed to look at us, too, as if we were the ghosts, remnants of another world they were just entering. In their eyes, we could see the same spark we'd had not too long ago, the same curiosity tinged with fear. They didn't know yet, couldn't know yet, what all of this would feel like when it was their turn to leave. Arriving at the airbase the next day, a strange feeling hung in the air—a feeling we hadn't known for months. We were going home. For once, the mission wasn't forward, it was back, back across borders, back to familiarity. It felt strange and thrilling, like an unexpected gift. They allowed us to wash the layers of white dust from our faces, dust from the "Kaplyn." We scrubbed our faces until we could finally see our own skin again in the mirrors.

## From Hippie to Preacher

One by one, we lined up for our bags to be checked, making sure we hadn't smuggled any foreign currency, stray ammunition, or enemy gear as "souvenirs." The MPs went through everything with hawk-like eyes until they were satisfied we hadn't brought the war back home with us. Finally, the signal came—times to board the Flossie.

We boarded the Flossie, our eyes wide open with excitement. The hum of the engines, once an endless drone that dulled our senses, now seemed almost cheerful as it carried us closer. We swapped stories, chatting and laughing above the steady thrum, talking about what we'd do once we set foot on solid ground. Some boasted they'd head straight to the bar and drink until they couldn't remember their own names; others talked of university plans or signing up for the permanent force.

From Hippie to Preacher

Most of us were lost in thoughts of the things we'd finally buy with our hard-earned danger pay. Dreams of new watches, fancy clothes, maybe a car or bike flashed through our minds, and the conversations flowed with it— small talk, plans, laughter. Then, suddenly, the engines shifted tone, signalling we were descending. A ripple of excitement ran through us. Flossie began its slow turn, angling to face the wind for landing. As the wheels touched the ground, an unstoppable cheer broke out. We'd made it.
Final orders came quick and clipped. Grab your kit, fall in line, and follow the lieutenant. We marched off the ramp in the cool twilight, a line of silhouettes trudging towards the storerooms of the army base. There, we would "clear out"—hand in our rifles, sign the last paperwork, and finally collect our pay

packets. The feel of that packet in hand, full of danger pay and every outstanding cent, was almost too good to be real. Some of us, who didn't have cars waiting or family nearby, collected train tickets for the journey home. We said our goodbyes, hearty slaps on backs and grins all around. Just as we thought it was time to part ways, Koos, looking distressed, cracked us all up. Turns out he'd left his car with his girlfriend's brother in Orkney. But now he was stuck here in Bloemfontein, halfway across the country. "Its fine," he muttered, "only three hundred kilometres!" We couldn't stop laughing, but luck was with us that night. An officer overheard and offered Koos and a few of us a lift to Welkom since he was headed to Kroonstad. As we piled into his car, the final memories of this long, strange journey lingered, the laughter, dust, and twilight blending together as we sped into the

night, finally on our way home. The cool night air brushed against my skin, the lingering warmth from my brisk walk keeping me just on the edge of comfort, neither hot nor cold. I pushed open the little gate, the rusty hinges creaking with a sound that echoed through the quiet. A curtain flicked aside in the window, and, as if on cue, every light in the house sprang to life, bright and welcoming. The front door flew open, and there was, my eldest sister, with a huge grin on her face, shouting my name. Behind her, my younger siblings pushed and scrambled, each trying to be the first to reach me. They crowded around, pulling me into a flurry of hugs and laughs. Tony grabbed my bag from my shoulder with a grin, while Paul stood wide-eyed and speechless, excitement bubbling over so fast he stuttered his hello.

From Hippie to Preacher

And then there she was, my mom, standing a little back, her eyes bright and teary. She waited patiently, letting the kids get their hugs in, and when they finally stepped aside, she opened her arms to me. I stepped into her embrace, feeling her warm hands cradle my back as if she could never let me go. The knot in my throat tightened as I swallowed, and her tears mingled with a soft smile as she held me close, neither of us needing words. Once the commotion settled, I slipped into the kitchen and sat at the old, familiar table. I barely had to ask before a glass of water was placed in front of me, though everyone's attention was now chattering at once, filling me in on every little detail I'd missed. When I finally managed to get a word in, I asked, "Where's Dad?" "Working the night shift at the mine," Stutters Paul. And are you working the day shift I ask?

From Hippie to Preacher

Paul looked at me, his face all earnest, and he laughed with the others. "No, man! I don't work!" he said, shaking his head. The laughter filled the room, and before we knew it, midnight had crept in. One by one, we all yawned and stretched, the thrill of the reunion fading into warm exhaustion. Tony offered to help with my bag, and I followed him out to the little room outside, a cosy nook with fresh sheets and a faint smell of lavender hanging in the air. I thanked Tony and went to shower, letting the warm water wash away the remnants of the road and the military life I'd stepped away from, at last. When I finally slipped into bed, the room quiet around me, I let out a deep breath. Home, I thought, letting the word settle. It felt good. That morning, I woke to the soft trilling of birds, their songs weaving through the open window, blending with the first hints of morning light. I lay there

for a moment, absorbing the familiar sounds, until I heard the crunch of gravel under my dad's tires as he pulled into the yard. I jumped out of bed, quickly pulling on my army PT shorts and an old t-shirt. Barefoot, I stepped out into the backyard, meeting him halfway to the back door. "My, oh my," he said, breaking into a smile. "Look who's here." His arms wrapped around me, and we hugged the way fathers and sons do when words feel too small. "When did you get here?" he asked. "Late last night." The sun had already nudged its way over the horizon, casting a warm glow over the yard. Just then, the door swung open, and there stood my mom, beaming at us both. "Morning!" she said, leaning over to give my dad a quick kiss before ushering us inside. She'd already poured a steaming cup of coffee for him and offered to pour one for me, too, as she bustled around, packing lunches for the

## From Hippie to Preacher

younger kids. While she assembled the sandwiches, Dad and I caught up over our coffee, our words easy, familiar. "Would you sign for me again, Dad? I'm still not 21," I said, breaking the gentle quiet. He looked up. "What do you want to buy this time?" "A bike," I said. "But first, I'll need to see what the shops have in Welkom. Koos, who was in the army with me, mentioned there are three or so shops here." Dad nodded thoughtfully. "You still need to stop by Blyvoor mine and ask for a transfer so you can finish your trade. Once you've got transport, though, that should be easier." "Exactly," I replied, feeling the familiar pull of my next steps, decisions big and small. Just then, Paul walked in, his gangly frame filling the doorway, grinning as he announced he had only one month of school left. "Wow, you're getting old!" I teased, clapping him on the shoulder.

## From Hippie to Preacher

Mom chimed in, "Down at the end of the street, there's a bus stop. Buses come every two hours from 6 to 6." "Thanks, Mom. I'll catch one in a bit, see if I can find myself a bike," I said, nodding gratefully. Dad and I moved into the living room, settling down in the well-worn armchairs. He leaned back, looking at me thoughtfully. "Tell me, son, how were your days on the border?" I swallowed, finding words hard to gather. There were things I could say and things I couldn't—or maybe just didn"t want to. As the house began to fill with the warm, comforting smell of toast, Dad nodded, understanding without asking too much. "Welcome home, my boy," he said, his voice full of warmth and quiet pride. I smiled, feeling the weight of his words settle somewhere deep. "Thank you, Dad." Soon, the younger ones filtered in, grabbing their sandwiches and backpacks,

each stopping to say goodbye before heading out to catch the bus to school. Their footsteps faded down the lane, and for a moment, the house was still, filled only with the quiet hum of home. Later, I found myself waiting at the bus stop, rocking a pair of faded bellbottoms and my well-worn Moses sandals. Wearing civvies felt strange, like stepping into someone else's skin. Standing there, I kept my weight on one foot, avoiding the rough wooden plank—no way I was risking dirt on my freshly laundered pants. It has been washed and ironed. And every little thing, even sitting on a bus stop bench, felt oddly new. Soon enough, I spotted the bright blue bus cresting the hill, its engine humming with a faint growl. When the driver saw me, he slowed, his eyes flicking up and down as he took me in. With a soft hiss, the doors swung open, and he gave me a curious look.

From Hippie to Preacher

"New here?" he asked, voice warm and a bit gruff. "Yep," I said, stepping in, "Just finished my army service. "He nodded a flicker of understanding in his eyes. "Well, get in," he said, a smile tugging at the corners of his mouth as the door shut behind me. "How much?" I asked, reaching for my pocket. He just waved it off with a grin. "Next time," he said, "my treat. Least I can do." Grateful, I took the front seat, and we fell into an easy conversation, the kind you have with someone who already feels like an old friend. I mentioned I was in the market for a bike, and he perked up. After a few stops, he gestured through the window. "Look over there," he said, pointing to a big store across the road. "Best bike shop in Welkom. "I thanked him and hopped off the bus, barely feeling the steps beneath my feet.

# From Hippie to Preacher

And then, there it was. Love at first sight. The Kawasaki Z1300. I'd heard tales about this beast back in the army, but I never imagined it would look *this* good in real life. "Wow," I muttered, crossing the distance as if in a trance. I couldn't hear the shop's radio or the faint chatter around me; it was just me and the bike. In my head, I was already racing down open roads with it. "Will you marry me?" I asked, only realizing I'd spoken out loud when I heard a laugh. "Excuse me, sir?" The salesman stood beside me, grinning from ear to ear. "Ah—I, uh, I was talking to my Kawa," I said, feeling a bit sheepish. His grin only grew wider. "Well, she's for sale if you're serious." "How much for the deposit?" I asked, unable to keep the excitement from my voice. He led me to the desk, papers everywhere, the scent of new tires and petrol filling the air, and I realized that everything I'd been waiting for

was here the sun had slipped behind a thick cloud, casting a grey veil over the world as I stepped out of the bike shop. But even in the dimmed light, my heart was still alight with the thrill of seeing the Kawasaki Z1300 up close. The sleek, aggressive lines, the way the metal gleamed, the quiet power in that engine... I had fallen for it the moment my eyes landed on it. But as I made my way to the bus stop, reality hit. That bike was out of my reach, no question. The price was steep, and my deposit wouldn't make a dent. Even the down payment alone was more than I could stretch to right now. So, with a sigh, I made up my mind: I'd wait, save up, and someday, I'd have it. The Kawasaki was a dream on hold, but it wasn't going anywhere. For now, though, my plans needed to be more practical. I'd ask my dad to take me to Blyvoor so I could sort out the transfer

paperwork for moving from that mine to a job in Welkom. Being new here, there wasn"t much I knew—nobody, really, except for Koos, a buddy from the army who lived here somewhere. So, heading home felt like the only option. When the bus finally pulled up, I noticed the driver was different from the one who'd brought me here. "Fairbairn Street, Dagbreek," I said, and he nodded, confirming the fare as R2. I fished out the coins, watching through the window as cars zoomed by. After six long months on the border, just being back on civilian streets again felt surreal. This town was new to me, and it made me feel strangely adrift. As the bus wound its way through the streets, I felt a subtle shift inside, a quiet thrill that replaced the familiar sense of displacement. The quiet neighbourhoods and curving streets seemed to whisper possibilities.

Back home, I sat at the kitchen table, biting into a piece of toast slathered with jam. The house was quiet, which was rare. I told Mom all about my bus ride into town and the stop I'd made at the bike shop. I could tell she appreciated the company—Dad was still asleep from his night shift at the mine, and everyone else was still at school. Mom listened closely, nodding as I talked. When I mentioned that my heart was set on a bike, she sighed. "A car is so much more practical, Sean," she said, brushing a stray crumb off the table. "Maybe," I replied, feeling the excitement rise again, "but after seeing that Kawasaki Z1300, I can't think of anything else. Nothing else even comes close." The look on her face was somewhere between worry and reluctant acceptance. She knew me well enough to realize my mind was mostly made up.

We talked a while longer, and she mentioned Paul finishing school next week. It was hard to believe the year had gone by so fast. And it was strange to think my year of army service was done too, a week ahead of schedule. Before long, the front door flew open. "Hello, Mom! Hello, Sean!" It was Tony and Dot, the first of the school crowd arriving home. Then came our two other sisters, laughing and chattering. Finally, Paul appeared, carrying his bag over one shoulder and looking half as tired as Dad had after his shift. After a while, I slipped away to my room out back. I put on a record, thinking I'd play some music and unwind, but Paul followed me, pushing open the door and flopping onto the bed. "So, did you find a bike?" he asked, looking at me expectantly.

"Yes and no," I replied. "I saw the Kawa Z1300." I felt a grin creep over my face. "It's perfect. But way out of my price range." Paul raised an eyebrow. "So why not buy something else, just for now? Save up until you can get the one you want." "Yeah, maybe," I said, though I wasn't sure. "I'll look around more tomorrow." Right then, Tony poked his head through the door, grinning. "Hey, Sean, play *Summer Holiday*!" I rolled my eyes. "Not yet, Tony! you've got a week left of school!" But I put it on anyway, and soon enough, there we were, the three of us singing along to Cliff Richard. Our voices tumbling over one another, laughing too hard to hit any of the notes. Saturday morning dawned bright and beautiful, sunlight spilling through the thin curtains, casting soft, golden rays across the room. It looked to be a

# From Hippie to Preacher

promising day. Just as I began to stretch and sit up, there was a knock at the door.
"Coming!" I called, getting to my feet as the door creaked open. There stood Dad, looking weary yet warm, fresh from his night shift. His face was lined with fatigue, but he still managed a gentle smile. "Hi," he greeted softly. "Your mom told me yesterday... you didn't have much luck at the bike shop? "I gave a small nod. "Hello, Dad. Yeah, the bike I want is just... it's too expensive." He sighed, a knowing look in his eyes. "Yeah, sometimes we want things that just aren't meant for us," he said thoughtfully. But I could feel the stubborn determination rising in my chest. "But, Dad," I replied, unable to hide my excitement, "that's *the* bike. I've heard about it, you know, from guys in the army. And then, when I finally saw it—it was love at

first sight." My voice grew eager. "That Kawasaki Z1300... it"s a beast!" Dad chuckled at my enthusiasm. "I know, I know." He ruffled my hair affectionately. "I've got the day off till Monday afternoon. Monday morning, I'll take you to Blyvoor so you can put in for a transfer to one of the mines over here in Welkom." I felt a surge of gratitude. "Thanks, Dad." I knew this would make things easier for us as a family, being closer together. "Me and Paul are heading into town this morning, though, just to look around at some of the other bike shops... who knows what we'll find?" "Good plan," Dad said with a smile, standing up. "Enjoy the outing. Now get dressed, and we can have some breakfast." And with that, he gave a little wave before heading back down into the court yard, leaving me grinning with the thrill of what the day might bring.

From Hippie to Preacher

As Paul and I stood at the bus stop, a thick, warm wind tugged at the loose ends of our shirts, whipping them against our arms. Paul had just a week left of school, and I couldn't help but feel a little strange, standing there with him, almost like we were waiting for the same bus but headed for different places entirely. "So, where are you gonna work?" I asked, more out of habit than anything. Dad had brought him some papers last week—an application for an apprenticeship as a boilermaker, and it seemed like everything was already lined up. Paul gave a half-smile, his eyes skimming the empty road. "Dad handed it back in already," he replied, shrugging. We kept up the kind of idle chatter brothers share—weather, what Mom might make for dinner—until the bus finally rounded the corner and rolled to a stop in front of us. We climbed aboard, and I made for my usual

## From Hippie to Preacher

seat, pressing my face against the cool, slightly dusty glass of the window. Outside, rows of mine houses flashed by, neat and solid, with their little brick walls and tended lawns. They looked far better than the weathered, fading mining village where we grew up. I felt a strange tug in my chest as I watched them pass, like I was looking at a world I might never quite belong to. The bus slowed again at the next stop, and a boy about Paul's age climbed on. "Hello, Paul," he greeted, flashing a grin. Paul smiled, nudging my shoulder with his. "That's Mark," he whispered, gesturing at the boy. "He's in the same class as Sis." Mark came over, his gaze flicking between us with that easy confidence of a kid who knows he belongs. Paul introduced us. "This is Sean, my eldest brother," he said, sounding strangely formal. Mark nodded, recognition sparking in his

# From Hippie to Preacher

eyes. "Oh, Sis told me about you," Mark said, then turned to Paul. "Where're you headed?" Paul explained, and Mark, with a quick nod, asked if he could tag along. Apparently, he'd been over at his friend Jonny's house, but no one was home. The neighbours said they'd all gone fishing at Blaudrift the main fishing spot here in Welkom. I remembered my Uncle Corrie who use to lived her but are back at Blyvoor. He loved to fish, or maybe the alcohol that goes hand in hand with fishing. With Mark along, it felt like we had our own tour guide; he knew the town in a way Paul and I didn"t yet. When the bus came to a halt again, Mark was the first on his feet. "We better get off here," he said, pressing the bell before leading us down the narrow aisle. "The bike shop's just behind that tall building over there."

From Hippie to Preacher

We stepped off the bus, our feet hitting the pavement with a quiet thud. For a moment, I just looked up at the buildings stretching toward the sky, feeling the pull of something bigger, wondering if Paul felt it too. The three of us approached the bike shop, and as soon as we got close, the deep hum of engines hit us, loud and rhythmic. The smell of exhaust hung in the air, sharp and oily, filling the shop like an invisible fog. But we pushed through, undeterred, stepping into a world of gears, tools, and steel. Inside, bikes lined the walls, each one bearing a different history, the dings and scratches speaking of miles and memories. There were second-hand models—small, sturdy 50ccs, a few sleeker 100cc and 250cc options, and a 380cc Suzuki that caught my eye. But it was the brand new Honda 500 Four that stopped us in our tracks.

# From Hippie to Preacher

Glossy and fierce, it gleamed under the harsh fluorescent lights like a prize waiting to be claimed. In the corner, a mechanic was hunched over a 900 Kawasaki, revving its engine to a throaty roar. "This one's in for a tune-up," he shouted over the noise, glancing up briefly. "Belongs to a client." We hung around a few more minutes, watching him work, each rev sending a shiver down my spine. It made me crave my own set of wheels even more. But I knew my heart was set—I'd wait for the Z1300. Once outside, I turned to Mark. "Know any other bike shops around here?" I asked. He shrugged. "Nah, just a repair place over in St. Helena. Not much to see." "Alright," I said, nodding. "Let's head over to the Horseshoe." The Horseshoe was the heart of our small town, a semi-circle of shops and cafes that formed the main strip.

## From Hippie to Preacher

For anyone new, it was where the action happened—small restaurants that served coffee strong enough to jump-start anyone's day, little boutiques, and the OK Bazaars anchoring it all. OK Bazaars had everything you could want: furniture, clothes, and groceries. But today was a Saturday, and that meant I was treating my brother and his friend Mark to the real deal—pies, chips, and gravy, washed down with ice-cold Pepsis. We wolfed down our meal, savouring every bite, the perfect fuel before we decided to tackle the long walk back to Dagbreek. Buses could get us there quicker, but there was something better about walking, just moving one step at a time, talking as the sky faded from blue to purple. As we walked, I got to hear more about Mark's life. Turns out, he had a sister who was just about to finish standard 9. "She makes the best cake in Welkom," he bragged, eyes

From Hippie to Preacher

lighting up. "Really?" I grinned, thinking it might be worth finding out if that was true. "Yeah, maybe next time I can bring you some. She'll be baking up a storm after exams are over. "And with that, the three of us kept on walking; leaving the day behind us and laughing as the house came into our sight.

Monday morning came before we were fully awake, but we were already on the road by first light. It was me, my dad, and Paul—who'd taken the day off school, not that it mattered much since it was his final week and exams were behind him. The sun had barely tipped over the horizon, casting long shadows on the road ahead. Mom had packed a flask of coffee and sandwiches for us, and Dad was keeping an eye on the time, as he'd need to be back by 2 o'clock for his afternoon shift.

From Hippie to Preacher

Our goal was simple: get to Blyvoor by eight, finish up by ten, and make it back to Welkom just in time for Dad's work. Small talk filled the car, a few stories about Paul's last days at school, and Dad tossing in his usual dad jokes here and there. The familiar sights rolled past, and when we crossed the Vaal River, we stopped to stretch our legs and have a quick bite. The coffee was perfect, warm and strong, and we stood there for a few minutes watching the river, which had turned to a burnished orange under the morning sun. Fish splashed at the surface now and then, sending ripples out into the calm water. There was a quietness to it all, an unhurried stillness that somehow made me both more aware of the moment and eager to get on the road. After packing up, we climbed back in and drove on, speeding past Orkney, then Potchefstroom, and finally turning off onto the gravel road

that led to Blyvoor mine. Dad checked his watch as we pulled up, smiling with satisfaction; we'd made it with five minutes to spare. Paul stayed in the car, while Dad and I headed inside. The mine office had a worn-down look, a mix of hard use and the kind of age that creeps into places left mostly the same year after year. Mr Roberto, the personnel officer, greeted us, his glasses balanced on the end of his nose. "So, finished with the army?" he asked, looking me over. "Yep," I replied, trying to keep things polite and straightforward. After exchanging a few words with Dad, he got straight to the point. "So, what can I do for you?" I took a breath. "I'm here to ask for a transfer—to the Welkom mines." Mr Roberto" face fell slightly as he shook his head. Blyvoor isn't affiliated with the other mines," he said firmly. "It's not possible." Dad and I exchanged glances. The

weight of the trip and the hope we'd carried with us seemed to settle heavily in the small office. Mr Roberts must have sensed it because he pulled Dad aside into another room, leaving me to stew for what felt like ages. Eventually, they returned, and Mr Roberto handed me an envelope. Inside, I found my record of service, neatly folded, along with a few other documents. "Your dad's got to pay a fine for breaking the contract," he said, almost apologetically. "But go ahead and pick up your tools at the workshop. I'll call Louis." The ride back was lighter. We couldn't help laughing about Uncle Louis, who, as Dad recounted with a grin, had joked that he'd never wanted to see me again. The time passed quickly, and before we knew it, we were pulling back into Welkom with an hour to spare. Dad took a last

swig from the coffee flask, grinning as he got ready to head to the mine.
That Friday felt electric, the air buzzing with excitement as kids poured out of school, their voices filling the streets like a wave. It was the last day before the holiday break, and everyone, from the youngest kid to the oldest teacher, seemed to have caught the spirit. My younger brother Paul, finishing school for good today, looked especially thrilled. He was all set to start working, and with his savings, he planned to buy a Ford Granada—his dream car. The Ford had become more than a car to him; it was freedom, adulthood, the open road.
"See you later!" Paul's friends called out, clapping him on the back, their voices overlapping in a happy jumble. They had plans to hit The Horse Shoe, the main hangout in our small town of Welkom. Even with its

## From Hippie to Preacher

dusty streets and modest buildings, Welkom felt warm and familiar, the kind of place where everybody knew everybody. Dad stood outside, watering the garden with the hose in one hand, a cigarette balanced in the other. Mom wouldn't let him smoke indoors, but he didn't seem to mind. It gave him an excuse to be alone for a few moments, gazing off into the fading light as he smoked, lost in his thoughts. Fridays in Welkom were special for another reason, too—the *Vista*, our free local newspaper, would come. I waited eagerly for it, hoping to spot any job openings, my eyes scanning for something good. Dad's friend from work had mentioned that Orbit Engineering was looking for apprentice boilermakers. It sounded promising, so I kept my fingers crossed, hoping the paper would arrive before Dad headed off to his afternoon shift.

From Hippie to Preacher

Around noon, Dot and Tony burst through the door first, chatting excitedly about the start of the holidays. My sisters followed, chattering just as loudly. But Paul wouldn't be back until later, wrapped up in his own celebration. Finally, as Dad was leaving, the *Vista* arrived. I pounced on it, flipping through to the classifieds. My heart jumped when I spotted the ad in bold letters: *Urgent. Apprentice Boilermakers Wanted.* I couldn't believe my luck. I lay back on my bed, grinning, and the strains of the Bee Gees playing softly in the background. There was a whole new world waiting out there, and for the first time, it felt close, real, and within reach. I'm up before the dawn, the sky still cloaked in night. My head won't let me sleep, thoughts of the day racing through it.

From Hippie to Preacher

It's Monday, and today's not just any day— it's the day Dad takes me to Orbit Engineering. I've packed my big wooden toolbox, the one I got when I first started at Blyvoor Mine as a first-year apprentice. Today, I'm taking it to Orbit, just in case they decide I can start right away. As the sun begins to rise, it splashes hues of pink and orange across the clouds. The house is stirring, my siblings already awake, voices ringing through the summer air. They're on holiday, laughing and singing as they play in the early light. After a quick breakfast of pap, Dad, my little brother Paul, and I pile into the car. Dad takes a few back roads, winding through Welkom, until we finally pull up in front of a nondescript building. I can already hear the sounds of grinding, hammers, and the distant shouts of men at work. "This is it," I say to Dad, the thrum of activity beyond the walls

# From Hippie to Preacher

adding weight to the morning. Clutching my paperwork, I step inside. The secretary, a no-nonsense woman, ushers me to a chair and gestures for me to wait. After what feels like an eternity of watching the clock tick, I'm finally called in. The office is cluttered, papers and plans strewn across the large desk where a broad-shouldered man sits, his gaze fixed on me as I enter. "Fresh out of the army?" he asks, studying me with an appraising eye. "Yes, sir. And I've completed two years of apprenticeship at Blyvoor," I reply, keeping my voice steady. "Why'd you leave there?" he asks, leaning back, arms crossed. I explain that my family relocated to Welkom while I was in the army, and when I asked Blyvoor about a transfer, they couldn't accommodate me. I had no choice but to leave. The man nods, and then asks for my records. I hand him the folder, and he thumbs through it slowly,

carefully. "Would you be willing to travel from next year?" he asks finally. "We don't need it right now, but from your fourth year, you may have to go out to install equipment on-site." "No problem," I assure him, eager to make it work. He nods, more to himself than to me, then picks up the phone, calling someone from the workshop. "You'll start as a third-year apprentice," he says, explaining how they build custom equipment here and then send the team to install it for clients. "You'll be sleeping in a company caravan when you're out on the road." "That's fine by me, sir," I reply, my heart pounding with excitement. Just then, the office door opens, and a man with broad shoulders and a rugged face steps in. I stand, offering him my hand. "Sean, meet Uncle Hans, the workshop foreman," the boss introduces us. "Hans, here are his papers."

# From Hippie to Preacher

Hans nods as he skims my records, then glances at me with a quick nod of approval. "You can start tomorrow, seven sharp," he says. A smile spreads across my face. "Thank you, sir." Hans's eyes fall on my hands. "You've got tools? "Yes, sir, they're in the boot of my dad's car." "Good," he says, gesturing for someone nearby. "Ben, go help him carry his tools in."As Ben strides over, I thank the boss and follow Ben out to the car. I see Dad and Paul waiting, their eyes locked on me as I approach. "I'm starting tomorrow," I say, barely able to contain my grin. Dad's face breaks into a broad smile, pride beaming from him. Paul cheers, bouncing on his feet. I grab my heavy toolbox with Ben's help, and as we carry it in, he introduces himself. "Started last week," he says with a grin. Inside, Uncle Hans shows me a spot to stow my tools. "See you tomorrow," he says, clapping me on the

shoulder. I nod a rush of gratitude swelling within me as I step back outside. For a moment, I just stand there, taking it all in the sound of the workshop behind me, Dad and Paul waiting in the car. The road ahead stretches out, full of promise. Friday was payday at Orbit Engineering, and that meant the same thing every week: we got to head home at two o'clock. Everyone knew it, and everyone looked forward to it. But this Friday felt different. The anticipation wasn't just about the early finish—it was about what came next. For me, it meant a chance at freedom, or at least as close as I'd get. I'd spent the whole week carpooling with Uncle Hans, who had his routines down to an art. Every day from Tuesday on, he'd pick me up, and drop me off at the corner of my street, right near where Koos used to pull up when we were in the Army together.

# From Hippie to Preacher

It was funny, the same old corner and me just a few months later, with things feeling both the same and totally different. But today was different. Today, I was going to stop by the bike shop. There was a Kawasaki Z1300 there, sleek and powerful, and I was fully in love with it. All week, I'd been thinking about it, working out every rand and calculating it down to the last cent. The salary plus the overtime would cover it, plus my boarding payments to Mom. The only thing standing between me and that bike was Dad's signature. At 19, I could work and earn overtime, but signing a bike loan was still out of reach. "Don't look too eager," Uncle Hans grunted as we climbed into his pickup. He knew where I was headed, even if I hadn't told him. "They'll see it in your eyes and raise the price."

From Hippie to Preacher

"Thanks for the tip," I muttered, too distracted to play it cool. We drove down the main road, past shops, places I barely noticed now after a dozen trips. But as we neared the bike shop, I felt every meter tighten the anticipation in my chest. Uncle Hans gave me a nod as he pulled over, his own brand of approval. "Make it quick," he said. I hopped out and headed into the shop. The Kawasaki was still there, polished and waiting. My heart raced as I touched the cool metal, imagining myself on the road, free and fast. If I could get Dad's signature, that bike would be mine. And for once, it'd be more than a payday—it'd be a ticket to something new. The bike shop owner's face lit up as soon as I stepped through the door. He recognized me from my last visit and grinned from ear to ear, his smile so broad I could see the glint of his back teeth. "I see you're back!" he exclaimed.

From Hippie to Preacher

"Yep," I replied, feeling a surge of excitement. "I'm ready to put down the deposit. My dad will come by sometime during the week to sign the papers. Then I'll pick it up next Friday. "His grin somehow grew even wider, and he chuckled, clearing off a section of the cluttered counter. There was an old fuel tank resting there, along with a handful of greasy spanners and bolts. He scooped them up and set them aside, his hand patting around the crowded counter until he unearthed an ancient receipt book. "Aha, gotcha!" he muttered to it as if it were a slippery customer. He flipped open the book, his hands worn but deft, and then glanced at me as I counted out the bills— a small mountain of cash made up of my hard- earned army danger pay from six gruelling months up on the border, plus every bit I'd managed to save on top of that.

From Hippie to Preacher

 His fingers swept over the notes, tallying up the amount. Finally, he gave a satisfied nod. "Perfect," he said, beaming as he handed me the receipt. "She'll be all ready for you by next Friday." We shook hands, and I pocketed the receipt, feeling the weight of it like a promise fulfilled. With a final wave, I turned and stepped outside, where Uncle Hans was leaning against his truck, waiting patiently for me, squinting into the late afternoon sun. I crossed the lot toward him, anticipation buzzing under my skin—Friday couldn't come soon enough.

Friday evening had a softness to it, a warmth that filled our little kitchen as we sat crowded around the table, bowls of creamy *melk kos* steaming in front of us. Dad was just stepping out of the bedroom, buttoning up his work jacket, his face weary yet determined. It was

his last night shift of the week down at the mine. I watched him tuck his lunch bag under his arm and thought I'd better ask now. "Dad," I ventured, "could you go past the bike shop during the week? I've already put down the deposit, so I could pick her up next Friday when we get off early for payday. "Dad looked at me, raising an eyebrow, and gave a slow, thoughtful nod. "We'll see," he said, his voice steady. "You think you"ll manage those payments each month? Don't forget your boarding fee to your mother here." His mouth hinted at a smile. I grinned. "Yep, I worked it all out. I can handle it." Tony, my younger brother, perked up. "Hey, am I getting a ride on the bike?" He had that glint in his eye, that mix of hope and mischief. Before I could answer, Paul jumped in, shaking his head and grinning. "Forget a ride! I don't want a lift on that Kawasaki 1300—I want to take it for a

## From Hippie to Preacher

spin myself!" The whole table burst into laughter. Paul had never ridden anything bigger than a scooter. Mom laughed loudest of all and shook her head. "Paul, you can't even ride a bicycle!" she teased, and we all howled even more. Laughter was pouring out of us, filling the kitchen as Dad pulled on his boots. Dad, always a quiet presence, chuckled as he adjusted his cap. "By the way, I saw there's a vacancy for a diamond driller down at the mine. Paul," he said, turning to him, "looks like they filled all the apprentice boilermaker spots, but this job might suit you fine. You'd start as a trainee, and qualify in about six months." with the possibility of going overseas Paul's eyes lit up. "Serious? And overseas, too?" "Yep, same company's got sites overseas. Better get your passport ready." Dad's voice was casual, but he was watching Paul closely. "Might come sooner than you think."

From Hippie to Preacher

Paul was already dreaming big, leaning back with a proud grin. "I'll buy myself a Granada V6, just wait and see. And none of you are getting a ride—only Mom and Dad!" Well, that set us all off again. Everyone around the table started badgering him, asking why they couldn't ride in it. Even Dot, who was barely tall enough to see over the dash of any car, was protesting loudly, hands on her hips. We laughed long after Dad slipped out the door for his shift. The laughter lingered in the air, hanging over the table, binding us all together as a family. It was moments like these—full of teasing, big dreams, and shared hopes—that made the struggles feel lighter, made us forget, just for a little while, that some things we had to fight hard for. And, if I got my bike next Friday, I was certain I'd never ride alone. Uncle Hans brought the pickup truck to a halt in front of the bike shop, brakes squeaking as

## From Hippie to Preacher

he stopped. The afternoon sun hung high, casting a warm glow over everything, and the sky stretched wide without a cloud in sight. It was the perfect Friday to finally pick up my bike. I climbed out, and Uncle Hans leaned out of the truck, grinning. "Ride safe, and don't wreck that bike by showing" off," he said, his voice stern but with a twinkle in his eye. "Thanks!" I waved, watching as he drove away, then turned to head into the shop. My excitement was building until I walked in and didn't see my bike. My heart sank, and it must've shown, because the owner looked up from the counter and waved. "Don't worry, she's here, just in the back," he called, walking over. "It's easier for you to ride out that way anyhow, less crowded. "Relief washed over me, and my grin came back. "Thanks," I said, and as we walked toward the back, he pointed to a wall with helmets of all

colours and sizes. "Pick any helmet you like. It's included." I couldn't help but push my luck. "What about two?" I asked, a little too eagerly. He chuckled, shaking his head. "You're pushing' it, but... yeah, alright, just keep it between us, alright?" He winked, and I could tell he was as excited as I was. Then, there she was, my brand-new Kawasaki. The sleek body, the chrome, that beautiful 1300cc engine. The shop owner patted her side and raised an eyebrow. "This isn't a bike for the faint-hearted, kid. Look after yourself." I thanked him again, strapping on my helmet. As I turned the ignition and felt the engine rumble beneath me, goose bumps prickled up my arms and stayed with me as I eased out of the shop and onto the street. People turned to look, some even stopping mid-stride to stare as I rolled by, the bike gliding smooth as butter.

From Hippie to Preacher

At stop signs, I could feel their gazes fixed on that deep-green body and hear the murmur of admiration. By the time I reached home, my chest was buzzing with pride. I pulled up to the gate, revving the engine just once for good measure, and sure enough, Tony came running out to swing the gate open. His grin stretched so wide I thought his face might split. "Whoa!" he shouted, looking the bike up and down. Then Paul ran out, and all my sisters poured from the house, laughing and smiling, circling around me like I'd just returned from some great adventure. "It's too big for you!" one of my sisters teased. Tony didn't waste any time. "Can I sit on it?" he asked, already hopping from foot to foot. "Alright, but only for a second." I helped him up, and his little hands gripped the handlebars like he'd just landed on a spaceship.

# From Hippie to Preacher

Mom came out next, shaking her head but smiling, arms crossed. "Look at you," she said with a sigh, but she was proud, I could tell. She gave me a hug and a "Congratulations," while my siblings peppered me with questions and begged for their own turn. Only my eldest sister stood back, eyeing the bike warily. "That thing looks dangerous," she said, folding her arms. We all laughed, knowing she was right, but that's half the fun. With one last look at the Kawasaki, I waved them off, heading to my room to wash up. I could still feel the engine humming under my skin, like part of me was still out there, flying down the open road. After washing off the grit and sweat from the day's work, I headed into the kitchen, where Mom was already elbow-deep in flour and stock pots, preparing for dinner. She looked up and gave me a small, quick smile.

"Can you run down and grab some pies for tonight?" she asked, not pausing as she stirred. "I'll be making the gravy. But remember, your dad only eats steak and kidney, so get one of those for him. And pick up one for me as well. Cornish for the others and anything you like for yourself." Before I could reply, Tony came running over, practically bouncing with excitement. "I'm coming with you!" he declared, already fumbling for his helmet. I helped him fasten it, although it was still a little too big on his head, wobbling as he bobbed in place. He shot off ahead to open the gate, his little legs moving fast as he dashed to clear the path for my bike. As I turned the Kawasaki around and started it, our dog peered around the corner of the house, his ears back, watching us with nervous eyes. Tony swung the gate wide, and I gunned the engine, the bike rumbling as we rolled down the street.

# From Hippie to Preacher

The sounds of barking dogs and curious eyes followed us, heads turning as we rode past the neighbours' houses. When we finally turned into the horseshoe-shaped lot near OK Bazaars, two other bikers glanced our way. They straightened up, watching as I parked, and by the time I cut the engine, they were already strolling over. As Tony hopped off with a grin, I swung my leg over to meet the two strangers. They introduced themselves as Jonny and Vossie, both eyeing the bike with approving nods. "When'd you get the Kawa?" Jonny asked, patting the seat. "This afternoon," I replied, taking my gloves off. Jonny raised a brow. "You in any club?" I shook my head. "Nah, just got here, actually. Started working at Orbit Engineering." Jonny and Vossie exchanged a look. "Well, you're in luck," Jonny said, grinning. "We ride together every Friday. Club meets at St. Helena Hotel,

## From Hippie to Preacher

seven sharp. You ought to come by, see what you think." I shrugged, giving them a friendly nod. "Maybe I will." Inside the shop, Tony held his helmet under his arm, chin lifted like an old-school biker. I couldn't help but smile at how serious he looked, and we got a few smiles from passers-by who noticed him too. We made our way over to the warm glass case, picked out the pies Mom wanted, and grabbed a couple more just in case. On the way out, Tony looked up at me, eyes wide with excitement. "Next time, can I hold onto the handlebars?" I laughed, ruffling his hair. "We'll see, champ. We'll see."

Saturday at work, everyone had their eyes on me and my bike. The Kawasaki sat proudly in the parking lot, gleaming under the mid-morning sun. Even Hans, the foreman—who usually only ever noticed if you were ten

minutes late or left five minutes early—came over. He adjusted his cap, gave a low whistle, and said, "She's gorgeous." I couldn't help but smile, watching the crew gather around, each taking a closer look, firing off questions. They were captivated by her polished body, the sleek green curves, the way she caught the light just right. I didn't mind the attention. Saturdays were usually long, quiet shifts, stretching out till four. Days like this, when everyone was buzzing with something a bit out of the ordinary, broke up the routine. And anyway, it's the hours here that pay for the bike, so I couldn't complain. The ride home was the best part of the day. The sun was already low on the horizon, casting a golden hue across the road, and I felt that familiar longing for an open highway, one where I could ride clear and free without thinking about clocking back in come

From Hippie to Preacher

Monday morning. But that would have to wait—leave was still a long way off. When I pulled into the driveway, I saw Mark and Paul hanging out by the gate. Mark was here often, and though Paul wanted to do his apprenticeship as a boilermaker at Orbit, they didn't allow family members to work together. Something about avoiding complications, though it was a pity; Paul would've been a good fit. Paul waved and opened the gate as I rolled through, and as soon as I dismounted, Mark was at my side, letting out a whistle of his own. "Wow, that bike's a monster," he said, eyes wide. I just grinned, when I headed to my room out back to shower and clean up. My room was my own little corner of the world, with its own shower and toilet, giving me space to unwind.

# From Hippie to Preacher

When I came inside, freshly cleaned, I found everyone gathered in the kitchen. Mom was making stew and rice, the scent filling the whole house. Dad was leaning against the counter, chatting with her, but they both turned to greet me. After saying our hellos, Dad asked about the club that had invited me to join them. I shrugged, "It won't work, Dad. I'm tied up every day. Fridays, I get off at two, but Saturdays and Sundays are always four o'clock." Everyone lingered in the kitchen, and it felt good, all of us together. Then Paul chimed in with news that he'd be starting to work on Monday as a diamond driller at the same mine where Dad worked. Mom beamed, proud, but asked if I could go to town to grab some eggs for breakfast tomorrow. She knew how much I longed to take the bike out for any excuse.

From Hippie to Preacher

Just as I was about to go, Tony ran out with my helmet in hand, eager to come along. But before he could claim a spot, Paul stepped in, claiming it was his turn. Then, to everyone's surprise, Dad took the helmet, grinned, and said, "No, I'll go with him." Tony and Paul handed over the shopping bag, and with Dad clinging on, we took off. I rode slow into town, but on the way back, I let the Kawasaki roar a bit, feeling her power surge beneath us. By the time we pulled back into the driveway, Dad climbed off; pale-faced but laughing, saying he'd never get on that bike with me again. Everyone burst out laughing, even Mom, who had overheard and came to see what all the commotion was about. For a moment, with laughter filling the yard, it felt like everything I worked for was right here— both the thrill of the ride and the warmth of home.

# From Hippie to Preacher

The dinner table was filled with the usual banter and clatter of silverware, everyone's voices overlapping in the comforting chaos of a family meal. But Paul, who'd been uncharacteristically quiet that evening, suddenly cleared his throat and said, "Next month, I'm going to Middlesbrough." Silence blanketed the room. Even the clinking of forks against plates paused. Dad frowned, squinting across the table. "Where's that?" he asked. "In the UK," Paul replied, his voice both proud and nervous. "My foreman said the six months of training is officially done tomorrow and, well… I was chosen to go work at Teesside Drillcorp." I was the first to speak. "That's incredible news!" I managed, genuinely happy for him, though I could sense everyone else's mixed emotions, especially Mom's, as she stared down at her plate, her face thoughtful.

From Hippie to Preacher

Dad looked concerned but impressed. "Where are you going to stay?" he asked, with that practical glint in his eye. "They're putting us up in a hotel at first," Paul explained, "but this month I need to get my passport sorted." He looked down at his hands, as though realizing just how soon this big change was coming. "Isn't it crazy how fast six months gone by?" He shook his head, but then, unable to contain his grin, he said, "And the best part? The money I'll be making from this contract alone should cover a Ford Granada V6." We all laughed, and Sis jumped in, teasing. "You do know there's a whole ocean between here and the UK, right? You can't just drive that thing all the way back home!" We burst out laughing again, and even Dad joined in, his serious expression softening as he chuckled. "Maybe you ought to buy a boat instead, eh?"

From Hippie to Preacher

Paul just shook his head, laughing along with us. "Just wait and see," he replied, his grin stretching wider. Then, after a pause, Dad asked, "So how many of you are going from South Africa?" "We're four from here," Paul answered, "but there'll be others from different countries too." As the laughter settled, a quiet pride filled the room, mingling with a bittersweet sense of change. Paul was leaving, and though we'd miss him, we couldn't help but feel proud. It happened this past Friday, as the sun was high up in the sky. I'd just pulled up to the gate after a long day at work, ready to unwind, when I spotted a familiar figure approaching from the yard. Mark, a friend of Paul's, was with a young woman I hadn't seen before. "I'll open the gate!" Mark called, jogging over as I slowed the bike. I pulled in, parked, and climb off, glancing curiously at the girl beside him.

From Hippie to Preacher

Mark grinned, gesturing to her. "This is Sophia, my sister. We came to say goodbye to Paul—he's off tomorrow." I raised an eyebrow, suddenly intrigued. "Ah, is this the famous sister who bakes?" Mark's grin widened. "The best cakes in Welkom." Sophia, however, seemed unfazed by the small talk. Without a glance my way, she turned and started down the road. As she passed, I caught a glimpse of her profile—a gentle elegance framed by loose strands of hair. She looked like someone out of a storybook, the kind of girl who'd fit right in at a royal ball, but here she was, strolling casually past us. I watched her walk away, captivated, and gave a small, spontaneous smile. "Sophia, Sophia! Wait up, I'm coming!" Mark shouted as he hurried to catch up.

From Hippie to Preacher

Once they'd gone, I shook my head, chuckling at myself, and made my way inside, where a quiet flurry of activity greeted me. In the kitchen, Mom stood ironing a pile of clothes—Paul"s, I guessed. My brother's departure was set for tomorrow, and she wanted him to leave with everything neatly pressed and ready. Paul was chatting away, his words coming out in a steady stream as my eldest sister carefully helped him fold his shirts and pants, fitting everything neatly into his suitcase. I could tell he was excited, looking forward to the adventure ahead. Tomorrow, his company would pick him up, taking him straight to Johannesburg's airport. By evening, he'd be flying across continents with his colleagues, landing at Heathrow in the UK.

Dad wouldn't be home until ten tonight, working afternoon shift, so for now,

From Hippie to Preacher

The rest of us focused on getting Paul ready. I stayed for a moment, watching everyone move about the kitchen with a mixture of excitement and purpose, then slipped away outside to my room to freshen up. Still, I couldn't quite shake the thought of Sophia, her calm grace, her quiet presence. Little did she know that, in those few moments, she'd made quite an impression. And though I couldn't have explained why, there was a small, persistent feeling within me—that maybe, just maybe, I'd glimpsed something of my future in that quiet moment at the gate. The afternoon sun was beginning to dip as I tore down the road on my Kawasaki, pushing the 1300 cc engine with every turn. The bike roared beneath me, each vibration humming through my bones, reminding me that home wasn't far. But honestly, it wasn't home I was speeding toward.

From Hippie to Preacher

It was Mark's sister Sophia, who had stolen more than a passing thought since I'd seen her. Her name kept echoing through my mind like a tune I couldn't shake. *Sophia.* It felt like something out of a dream, too beautiful to be real. When I finally swung into the driveway, my thoughts were still miles away, with her. I parked the Kawasaki outside my room, where it usually slept, nestled under the window like a trusted companion. Just as I was shutting the engine down, I saw Tony, my young brother, sprinting over to close the gate behind me. "Hello, Sean!" he shouted, his voice bright and cheerful, with that endless energy only kids seem to have. "You're back fast today!" I grinned, unable to keep from sharing his excitement. "Yeah, got here as quick as I could." He ran a hand along the Kawasaki's sleek green and black frame, wide-eyed.

From Hippie to Preacher

"When are you gonna take me for a spin?" he asked with that look he always gave me, like he was asking for the world. "Maybe later, Tony," I laughed, walking towards the house. "But first I've got to clean up a bit. I'm covered in dust and soot from the shop." Between the welding, grinding, and cutting all day, a film of grime had settled on me, a gritty reminder of the work I'd just left behind. "Go and let Mom know I'll be out to greet everyone in a bit, yeah?" I told Tony as I headed toward my room. I needed to clear my head and shake off the day, let the black smudges from the machines and the weight of the week's labour melt away. I washed up, scrubbing at the dirt clinging stubbornly to my hands, my arms, even finding its way into my hair. And yet, with every wipe, every rinse, I felt lighter, like I was scrubbing off more than just grime. I was shaking off nerves, maybe

even preparing. Because after this, I'd make my way over to see her. Sophia. The thought made my heart beat faster than any machine in the shop. "You look sharp," Mom said, her eyes warm as she handed me a comb to tame a few stray hairs. I shrugged, giving her a quick smile. "Yeah, well... I thought I'd go over to see Mark for a bit." She glanced up from her stirring. "You think you'll be back for dinner?" The smell of her cottage pie was already drifting through the kitchen, cosy and inviting, the kind of scent that made you want to linger. I nodded. "I should be. Dad's back at six, right?" "That's the plan." She gave me a knowing look, one eyebrow arched. "Be back in time." "Thanks, Mom." I grabbed my jacket, throwing it over my shoulder. Today, I was leaving my Kawasaki parked. The last time Mark and his sister, Sophia, came over to send my older brother Paul off to the UK, she

## From Hippie to Preacher

didn't even look twice at my bike—or at me, for that matter. Still, something about her stuck with me. Mark and his family lived just around the corner, a short walk from our place. I spotted their front gate and paused as I saw Mark's dad standing outside. He looked over at me, a stranger to him.

"Is Mark here?" I asked, feeling a bit awkward. He raised his voice over his shoulder, "Mark! You've got company!" Mark emerged, grinning as he spotted me. "Sean! What're you doing here?" I shrugged again, trying to play it casual. "Just passing by. Thought I'd say hi." Truth was, I was hoping for a glimpse of Sophia. But I kept that part to myself. "Come on in. I'll introduce you properly," he said, leading me through the gate. "Dad, this is Paul's brother, Sean—the one who finished his service."

From Hippie to Preacher

Mark's dad gave me a quick nod. "Hello, Sean," was all he said before going back inside. We made our way through the house and into the living room, where Mark's mom came out from the kitchen to meet me. "Are you Paul's brother?" she asked, wiping her hands on a dish towel. "Yes, ma'am." My eyes darted to the hallway, and just then, Sophia walked past, heading toward her room. She didn"t even look my way. Mark caught the direction of my gaze, smirking as he noticed. "Come on, let's go outside," he said, steering me toward the door. Once we reached the gate, he leaned in, lowering his voice like he was letting me in on a secret. "Sophia's finishing up her last year. She'll be done with matric soon," he said, nudging me. I tried to play it cool. "Yeah? That's great."

From Hippie to Preacher

"You should come over next Saturday evening," he continued. "Dad works the night shift—leaves at seven. We can put on some records in the lounge and hang out." "What time's he usually off?" I asked, making mental notes of the plan. "Seven o'clock sharp, every evening." I nodded, grinning. "Sounds good. I'll be here." Walking back home, my thoughts drifted to Sophia. There was something about her that I couldn't shake. I whistled a tune as I crossed into our yard, feeling lighter than I had in weeks. My little brother, Tony, ran out, tugging on my sleeve. "Sean, you forgot your bike! "I laughed, ruffling his hair. "Yeah, I did." The next day I stood outside the gate, my Kawasaki rumbling beneath me as Tony sprinted out to unlatch it, grinning even before he got close. "Sean, Sean!" he called, waving me in before I'd even killed the engine.

# From Hippie to Preacher

"Mom got a letter from Paul!" I nodded, curiosity sparking. "What's he saying?" "Mom's waiting to read it when Dad wakes up. He's on the night shift." Tony grinned, unable to hold his excitement. "And believe it or not, the post office actually delivered!" "That's something," I chuckled, thinking of the long waits we usually endured. I swung off the bike, patting Tony on the shoulder. "I'll clean up and be over in a bit." My small room at the corner of the yard was my sanctuary, a little retreat from the bustle of the main house. The perk? I could leave my dusty boots and greasy overalls outside, no need to track through Mom's kitchen. Stepping into the shower, my mind wandered to Sophia, Mark's eldest sister, who would be writing her final exams soon. The thought of the future—her by my side, a place of our own—brought a smile to my face.

# From Hippie to Preacher

However, I quickly tempered my excitement. Sophia barely looked my way; it was more of a daydream than anything else. After drying off, I headed to the kitchen, where the scent of Mom's pasta filled the room. Plates and silverware were already set. Mom greeted each of us as we filtered in, and then Dad, freshly up and in his uniform for another night at the mines, joined us As we settled into our usual small talk, Mom finally held up the letter, her eyes bright. "It's from Paul," she said, her voice laced with excitement. Dad's face lit up, and my eldest sister leaned in. "Read it, Mom!" she urged. Mom reached for the letter she'd tucked on the fridge, carefully unfolding it.
"Hello, family," she began, her voice warm as she read Paul's words. "We're staying at a place called the Fox and Hounds Country

Hotel. We're on twelve-hour shifts, and most days it's either raining or bone-cold. Underground's warm, but up here, it's all damp and chill. In our downtime, it's darts and snooker." Mom's face softened at the next line. "Mom, I miss your cooking." She looked up at us, pride shining in her eyes. "The English can't cook like you," she read, and Dad chuckled. Paul wrote about how expensive everything was, even saying that Coke cost more than beer. We all burst out laughing at that, imagining Paul and his mates grumbling as they paid for their meals. "We often go to work with headaches," he wrote, which had everyone at the table grinning knowingly. Dad leaned back, shaking his head with a satisfied smile. "Paul's grown up. Gone off, become a man." My sisters laughed, and the conversation quickly turned to the V6 Ford Granada Paul had promised to buy once he

## From Hippie to Preacher

was back. We all pictured it gleaming in the driveway, our minds full of what-ifs and future plans. Mom gently folded the letter, placing it back on the fridge as if it were the most precious thing in the world. After dinner, Dad stood up, buttoning his jacket and grabbing his lunch box, and I walked him to the gate. We exchanged a few words about Paul, the mines, and the steady grind of work before he headed off. With the gates closed, I made my way back to my room, tossing on a record to let the Bee Gees harmony fill the space. A few minutes later, Tony and my youngest sister, Dot, came padding in, and soon the three of us were huddled by the stereo, singing along and sharing dreams—Paul's faraway life a reminder of everything that lay ahead.

# From Hippie to Preacher

I slipped my pay packet into my pocket, feeling the familiar crinkle of cash, and swung a leg over my Kawasaki. The roar of the engine seemed to sync with the rush in my chest as I pictured Sophia. Tonight, I'd see her—no more glances from a distance, no more waiting for the right moment. I'd stop by Mark's and finally, officially, introduce myself. I checked the time, calculating: just after 7, I needed to get there. By then, her dad would be off to work, pulling his permanent night shift down at the mine. I'd have a clear window, and I was determined to make the most of it. As I pulled up to the house, I spotted Tony at the gate, already waiting. I'd promised him a lift today, and since we had the luxury of an early 2 p.m. Friday knock-off, I figured we had time to kill before I needed to head out.

From Hippie to Preacher

I parked the bike, cutting the engine as Sis stepped outside, and calling, "Mom needs something from town." Inside, the faint creak of Dad's snores drifted from down the hall. He was finishing up his last night shift this week, starting mornings again on Monday. I stepped into the kitchen, Tony on my heels. "Hi, Mom," I greeted her. "Hello, Sean." She barely looked up from the potatoes she was peeling. "Could you run and get us some more potatoes? I was planning to make mash and minced." I nodded, "Sure, Mom." Tony was already by the door, clutching the spare helmet with a hopeful look. Back on the bike, we set off toward town, and as we rolled by Mark's place, I slowed, glancing over to see if maybe—just maybe—Sophia might be out front.

# From Hippie to Preacher

Nothing. I let out a quiet sigh and kicked up the speed. At the greengrocer, I grabbed a sack of potatoes and then remembered my plan. Sophia deserved something special tonight. I ducked into the Spar down the block and hunted down the biggest chocolate bar I could find. From across the aisle, I felt Tony's eyes on me, glued to the chocolate. He didn't even have to say a word before I relented, tossing a smaller bar his way. He flashed me a grin, catching the chocolate with both hands. "Thanks, Sean!" he said tucking the chocolate under his shirt as he hopped back onto the bike. By the time we reached home, I was chuckling to myself. Tony swung off the bike, and as he opened the gate, I caught sight of the chocolate bar, now a flattened mess, mushed from the ride. He looked down at the melted prize with wide eyes.

# From Hippie to Preacher

"You alright there, Tony?" I grinned, unable to hold back a laugh. He looked up at me sheepishly. "Guess I'll just eat it quick." As he tore into the bar, I thought of the night ahead. Soon enough, it'd be my turn to face the unexpected—tonight, under the stars, in front of Sophia's door.

Three years later lying on the narrow bed of our caravan, I hold Sophia's hand, and we dissolve into quiet giggles, reminiscing about the day we met. I offered her a chocolate, and she shook her head, pretending she didn't want it. So, I turned and handed it to her little sister instead, and that's when Sophia's resolve crumbled. She darted forward, snatching it from her sister's grasp, eyes alight with a mischievous gleam. "It's mine!" she declared, fiercely protective over something she'd just refused. I'd laughed so hard that her

mom came in, wondering what the commotion was all about. And Sophia? She punched me gently in the ribs, pretending I'd forced her into taking it. Who would have thought that a small moment like that—a bit of chocolate, a bit of laughter—would lead us here, 3 years later lying side by side in our little home on wheels, married for 1 year now. I turn to her, still marvelling. "Do you love me?" I ask, half-joking, half-serious. She clicks her tongue, smirking. "Can't you tell?" She places my hand on her growing belly. "Four months now, love." I smile, savouring the joy blooming between us. "What do you think? Boy or girl?" "Maybe it's a girl," she says, her eyes soft. "We could name her after you." "Sophia," I murmur, feeling the name like a blessing on my lips. "It's a beautiful name."

## From Hippie to Preacher

She squeezes my hand, her smile radiant in the dim light. Outside, the sun is dipping below the horizon, casting soft shadows over our caravan—a gift from Orbit Engineering when we got married, part of the deal for married couples stationed at the caravan park here at OD. They wanted us close, able to move where the job goes, and for now, it suits us. I'm a qualified boilermaker, and though the work takes us all over the country, we've got everything we need: our little house on wheels, a VW Beetle Sophia's dad gifted her when she passed matric, and my Kawasaki 1300, a bike that turns heads every time I take it out. Sophia's parents aren't exactly thrilled about us living in a caravan, but it's our home. My parents moved back to Carletonville; Dad's at Western Deep Levels now, and Paul's working over at Iscor in Vanderbijlpark after leaving diamond drilling.

# From Hippie to Preacher

Life's taken us all in different directions, but here we are, lying together on this quiet Sunday, hand in hand, talking about the past and the future and the love that holds it all together. Friday felt like any other day until the boss called me into the office with a grin on his face. "Big news," he started, shuffling a few papers on his desk. "We've landed a big contract in Richards Bay. You'll need to get all your tools ready and leave them with Uncle Piet. He'll be packing the trucks, getting everything loaded—welding machines, cutting torches, grinders, generators, you name it. Go home, pack your caravan; the van will hitch it up at 5 o'clock sharp tomorrow morning." " They've arranged a spot for you at the Aulusaf caravan park near Richards Bay. It should arrive by Saturday night or Sunday morning. And"—he held out a brown pay packet with a faint smile—"there's extra in here for a

## From Hippie to Preacher

Saturday night stay at the Richards Hotel." "How long's the contract?" I asked. "Two years, at the very least, maybe more. But it's solid work and good money."

I couldn't help the grin that spread across my face as I left the office. I was going to the sea! Richards Bay, a place I'd only dreamed about, now felt like it was calling me. The thought of two whole years by the ocean was surreal. After leaving my heavy wooden toolbox with Uncle Piet, I collected my pay packet and took a peek inside. R250 extra! That was a real treat, enough for a decent meal and a bit of a start to the new adventure. Pulling up to the caravan, I saw Sophia, just coming back from the ablution block with a load of freshly washed clothes. She looked surprised to see me.

# From Hippie to Preacher

"What are you doing home so early?" she asked, raising an eyebrow as she draped a shirt over her arm. "We're going to the sea," I said, unable to keep the excitement from my voice. "To Richards Bay! They're hooking the caravan at five tomorrow morning." Her eyes went wide, and then a slight frown crossed her face before her expression finally relaxed into a slow, blooming smile. "The sea?" I nodded, watching as the idea sunk in. Living by the ocean, something we'd both dreamed about for so long was finally happening. "Come on," I said, grabbing her hand, "let's tell your mom and dad before your dad heads off to work."

We climbed into the Beetle, Sophia at the wheel, and drove over. Her dad's face clouded when we shared the news, worry lines cutting across his brow.

## From Hippie to Preacher

"If you worked here on the mines," he said after a long pause, "you'd have a house, not a caravan. And you wouldn't have to travel around so much." The room went quiet. His words lingered, a mix of care and disappointment in his tone. He always hoped for something more stable, closer to home. Eventually, his gaze softened, and he gave a nod, just as Sophia's mom offered, "How about you both stay for dinner tonight? It'll be a while till we see you again." "Great," I said, nodding. "We'll head back, get our things in order, and be here a bit later." Back at the caravan, we packed everything down, making sure the tent was folded and secured, dishes wrapped so they wouldn't break, and clothes stowed neatly.

# From Hippie to Preacher

After a quick shower, we made our way to Sophia's parents" home, my mind already drifting to Richards Bay, to the sound of waves and salty sea air, knowing that we'd soon be waking up to that dream, together. Dinner at Sophia's parents' house was warm but tinged with an unmistakable heaviness, the kind that settles in when goodbyes are on the horizon. Sophia's mom, eyes filled with worry, reached across the table, her hand resting on Sophia's. "You're going so far away," she fretted, her voice catching. "Who's going to help you with the baby?" "Don't worry, Mom," Sophia replied gently, squeezing her mother's hand. "Everything will be fine."

## From Hippie to Preacher

I shifted in my seat, trying to bring some lightness back into the room. Turning to Sophia's dad, I asked, "Would it be alright if I left my bike here in the store behind the garage? Just until I can come back for it." He nodded without hesitation. "Of course. We'll keep it safe for you. I'll even take you to the caravan park on my way to work if you'd like." I thanked him, appreciating the ease with which he'd agreed. A little while later, he rose, hugged Sophia, and motioned for me to follow him out to the car. As we drove to the caravan, dusk settled around us, casting a soft orange glow over the fields. When we arrived, my bike was parked beside the caravan, glinting faintly in the last of the sunlight."Leave the keys in the kitchen with the others," he said as I hesitated, frowning slightly at the thought of leaving my Kawa behind. "Just in case I need to move it around

in the store," he added. Then, noticing my unease, he reassured me, "Don't worry, Sean. I'll look after it." I nodded, thanking him once more, and slipped the bike keys onto the hook inside as I returned. The ride back to their house was quiet, and by the time I arrived, darkness had settled in, casting the house in a cosy glow. Mark, Sophia's brother, had just gotten home from work on the railway and was waiting outside to help me push the bike into the storeroom.

"Look after my Kawa, alright?" I said to him as we maneuvered it inside. "Make sure nobody rides her. "Mark grinned and gave me a nod. "She'll be safe with me." Inside, the atmosphere was hushed, almost solemn. Sophia looked around the room, her gaze resting thoughtfully on her mom. "I think we should stay here tonight, in the spare room,"

she suggested. "The caravan's already packed, so we can say a proper goodbye in the morning." Her mom nodded in agreement, and I couldn't help but feel a weight lift from Sophia's shoulders. "Good idea," I said, giving her a reassuring smile. "You and your mom can chat while Mark and I go through some records." The mood lightened just a little as we settled in for the night. But in the morning, the gravity of leaving would settle again. For now, though, we savoured the warmth of family, the familiar sounds of home, and the knowledge that, soon, we"d be on our way. The road into Richards Bay had stretched long and busy, casting the afternoon in a haze that seemed to hang between sleep and waking. The late-day sun glinted off the road ahead as I fought to keep my eyes open, my mind slipping lazily between the lines of the pavement and the urge to just reach the

hotel. Sophia was next to me, grinning in the seat, and out of nowhere she started to laugh. I kept my gaze steady, glancing her way. "What's so funny?" She pointed out the window, where a sign rose from the marshy grasses, half-hidden behind thick green fronds. I slowed down to read it, squinting against the glare. "Watch Out for Crocodiles and Sharks," it said in big, stencilled letters. But then my eyes caught another sign just past it, clearly hand-painted, with a small tilt that gave it a slightly crooked appearance. "Watch Out for Crookediles and Sharks." We both burst into laughter, the kind of laugh that leaves your sides aching as we rolled toward the hotel. After parking the Beetle, we dragged our weary selves into the reception. I leaned on the counter, trying not to yawn as I asked, "Room for two?"

From Hippie to Preacher

The clerk handed us a key with a nod. "Breakfast included. And if you're looking to try something local, I can get a bunny chow prepared for you." Sophia's eyes lit up. Everyone back at work had talked about bunny chow like it was the holy grail of Natal cuisine, especially the mutton version. So we said yes, grinning at each other like kids in a candy shop. When we finally got to the room, Sophia all but collapsed onto the bed, too tired to do anything but kick off her shoes. I checked out the place, stowing our toiletries and pajamas, then wandered to the window. The curtains offered a narrow view of the bay, water sparkling in the twilight. Tomorrow, we'd explore, but for now, we were here, right where we wanted to be. A knock on the door snapped me back, and when I opened it, the porter stood there holding a steaming bunny chow on a tray. The smell of spicy curry filled

# From Hippie to Preacher

the room, and Sophia was up in an instant, joining me at the table. The "bunny chow" was a hollowed-out loaf of bread brimming with thick, aromatic curry, dotted with tender chunks of mutton. We dug in with curiosity and excitement, pulling pieces of bread to dip in the sauce.

As I took a bite, I stopped, my fingers brushing something hidden in the curry. "Sophia," I said, fishing out a leaf wedged between the meat, "look at this!" She leaned in, smiling, as I pulled out a thin, bark-like piece. I frowned, wondering if it had fallen in by accident. Feeling just a little unsure, I went to the reception desk, where the clerk promised he'd send the manager right up. The manager arrived soon after, a cheerful man with a quick smile, and looked at me with a polite nod. "Is there a problem?" I pointed to

## From Hippie to Preacher

the "leaves" and "sticks" scattered in our food. "Uh, these... it looks like someone cooked this under a tree or something," I stammered.
He stared, and then broke into a hearty laugh, clutching his stomach. When he finally caught his breath, he reached down, plucking up a leaf and munching it casually. "This," he said, holding up the evidence, "is a bay leaf. And this is a cinnamon stick." Sophia and I looked at each other, wide-eyed, before laughter overtook us too. The manager wiped a tear from his eye and, still chuckling, asked where we were from. "Welkom," I replied sheepishly. He shook his head with an amused grin. "A refund, then?" Blushing, I shook my head. "No, no—this bunny chow is perfect. I think we just needed a little schooling." The manager left us to it, and as we settled back into our meal, I couldn"t help but smile.

# From Hippie to Preacher

Here we were, tucked away in Richards Bay, eating "leaves and sticks," and somehow, it already felt like home. As we stepped out into the hotel foyer, a ripple of laughter spread across the faces of the staff. Every last one of them seemed to have heard the story about the "leaves and sticks" incident with our bunny chow—a misadventure that had somehow turned into a memorable joke. Sophia, beside me, was blushing all over again, her eyes avoiding the amused glances as we made our way through the lobby. "Come on," I chuckled, giving her hand a reassuring squeeze. "Let's go find the sea." She managed a smile, and with one last glance at the grinning staff, we walked out into the bright, open air. After a short drive, I parked the car, and we both climbed out, making our way down a sandy path toward the ocean.

From Hippie to Preacher

The sight of the water stretched wide before us, gleaming under the sun, took our breath away. "Wow, this is beautiful," Sophia murmured, her gaze fixed on the endless blue horizon. We kicked off our shoes, leaving them near the edge of the sand, and together we rushed forward, eager to feel the cool water on our feet. The sand was warm beneath us, yielding to each step until we finally reached the shore. Waves lapped up to greet us as we walked hand in hand, letting the gentle tug of the tide surround our ankles.
"This is the life," I said, breathing deeply. The tang of salt filled the air, sharp and bracing. Sophia, now four months pregnant, tilted her face to catch the breeze, but after a few minutes, she slowed, shifting her weight.
"Could we head back?" she asked, glancing down at her feet, which were starting to show

a fine dusting of sand. "The beach is getting a bit much for me." "Of course," I said. We made our way to a nearby tap, rinsing our feet beside the showers meant for surfers, then headed back to the car, refreshed and ready for the next part of our journey. Soon, we arrived at Aulusaf Caravan Park. Under a sprawling tree, I spotted our caravan, already set up and waiting. As we stepped out and opened the door, a small crowd began to gather—friends and colleagues from Welkom, people we knew well from our work at Orbit. They were here, like us, on contract, and it wasn't long before everyone was helping us get settled, extending cords to the nearest outlet and offering friendly advice. "Come join us for a braai later," one of them invited, and we eagerly accepted, grateful for the warm welcome. We were the youngest couple here, and that made

## From Hippie to Preacher

us a bit of a novelty among the others, who seemed ready to take us under their wing. As the sun set, we gathered around a blazing fire, the scent of wood smoke mingling with the aroma of roasting meat. And then, as laughter and conversation flowed, I decided to share our story—the leaves, the sticks, and the famous bunny chow. Everyone laughed—some so hard they wiped away tears. With every chuckle and shared smile, we felt the bonds grow stronger, ties woven through shared stories and warm camaraderie. In that easy moment around the fire, surrounded by new friends, we found the beginnings of a little community far from home. Every two months, we were granted a long weekend from Friday morning until Tuesday.

The rest of the time, it was twelve-hour shifts, Monday through Friday, and shorter hours on

# From Hippie to Preacher

Saturdays and Sundays. Despite the grind, the overtime made it worth it; in two weeks, we earned nearly as much as miners made in a month. I could hardly believe it, but somehow our first two months here in Richards Bay had flown by. Now we were finally headed to Welkom to visit my in-laws. Fridays had always held a kind of magic, but this one felt different. This time, the drive would lead us back to family. Sophia, now six months pregnant, wasn't exactly comfortable in the car, so I made sure to pack extra pillows and planned to stop frequently to let her stretch.

It was the era before cell phones, so we hadn't been able to warn the family of our arrival. We'd just have to surprise them. By the time we pulled up to my in-laws' house in Welkom, night had settled, casting shadows across the quiet street. As we turned off the engine, I saw

From Hippie to Preacher

Mark, Sophia's brother, already rushing out to meet us, his face lit up with a grin. He'd heard the car pull in, and as he jogged toward us, he called over his shoulder, "Sophia's here!" He greeted me with a hearty handshake. "Hello, Sean! Hello, Sophia," he said warmly, pulling her into a hug. One by one, the rest of the family appeared, drawn by the excitement. Only my father-in-law was absent; he was on the night shift and wouldn't be home until morning. After all the hugs and handshakes, and small talk while drinking coffee, we made our way to the spare room. It was past midnight, and exhaustion was settling in. As we crawled into bed, Sophia let out a soft laugh, shifting to find a comfortable spot. "You know," she murmured, "our bed in the caravan is more comfortable." We chuckled at the irony, and within moments, the weight of the day pulled us into a deep, contented sleep.

From Hippie to Preacher

The kitchen smelled of toast and marmalade, faintly warm and citrusy, as I sat at the table, biting into the crunchy crust and relishing the quiet before the day began. Then, with the creak of the back door, my father-in-law stepped in, looking worn but cheerful from his night shift. His eyes lit up as he saw us sitting there, especially when he spotted Sophia. She jumped up to greet him, and he beamed as he wrapped her in a hug. For a few minutes, we shared a simple, cosy breakfast, catching up in the soft morning light. When the plates were cleared, I leaned back and told them about my plan. "I'm heading over to Carletonville today to visit my folks," I announced. "Sophia's staying here, so I'll be back by tomorrow evening—Sunday night." I gave Sophia a nod; we'd talked about this on our drive back from Richards Bay yesterday.

## From Hippie to Preacher

"So," her dad said, turning to her with a grin, "how's life in Richards Bay treating you?" She broke into a smile. "Oh, it's wonderful. It's like we're living on a lifelong holiday." "Not for me, though," I interjected, rolling my eyes with a grin. "I'm working hard from morning till night. No holiday there!" Everyone laughed, and the sound filled the room, a pleasant hum of warmth. I stood up, glancing at Mark. "Mind helping me with the bike?" I asked. "It's tucked away in the shed, buried under a few things."
We made our way outside, where Mark helped me shift a lawn mower and a wheelbarrow out of the way. After some shuffling, my old Kawasaki 1300 stood free, coated in a thin layer of dust. I grabbed the garden hose, quickly rinsing off the grime until she sparkled like new. The bike gleamed under the morning

# From Hippie to Preacher

sun, promising miles of open road ahead. I took my helmet and jacket, turning to kiss Sophia. Her hand lingered on my arm for a moment, her eyes bright with a mix of excitement and worry. "Look after yourself," she murmured. "I will," I assured her, slipping the helmet on. Her father patted my back with a laugh. With a few hearty attempts, I got the Kawasaki roaring to life, the engine's rumble vibrating through me. I felt that familiar thrill course through my veins—a blend of freedom and pure, open-road exhilaration. As I revved the engine and looked back at them one last time, I knew the day ahead held nothing but a promise: the winding road, the roar of the engine, and that boundless feeling of adventure.

Riding out of Welkom early this morning, the sun blazed bright in the sky, casting golden

## From Hippie to Preacher

rays across the open road ahead. The promise of a new day hummed in the engine of my Kawasaki, a steady thrum of freedom that coursed through my veins. The world felt alive, and so did I, as I leaned into the wind, passing slow-moving vehicles with ease. Out of the corner of my eye, I caught a whirlwind dancing across a farm, swirling up dust and debris, snatching anything loose in its chaotic embrace. Farmers dotted the landscape, toiling with determination, preparing the earth for the sowing season that loomed just ahead. When I rode over the Vaal River, the sight took my breath away. The water shimmered like liquid gold, mirroring the morning sun. The beauty of it stirred memories, unbidden but welcome. I thought back to the time my dad, Paul, and I had stopped here for a quick bite on our way to Blyvoor. The laughter and camaraderie of that day still lingered in my mind.

From Hippie to Preacher

Another memory floated up, this one of Koos and me, halting at the very same spot on our way to the army base in Potchefstroom. Each moment seemed to intertwine with the river as if its currents carried fragments of my life downstream. But today, the journey was different. I was on my way to Carletonville to visit family. As the miles slipped by, I thought it had been wise to leave Sophia with her family for the weekend. The road offered solitude, a space to think and breathe. Just before noon, I arrived at my dad's place. Pulling up to the gate, I swung off the bike, its engine ticking softly as it cooled. Before I could unbolt the gate, a small figure came running towards me. It was Dot, the youngest, her face lighting up as she shouted, "Hi Sean! What are you doing here?" I dropped to her level and gave her a quick hug. "Surprise visit," I said, grinning.

From Hippie to Preacher

Tony appeared around the corner, his smile wide as he saw me. "Sean!" he called out, and we embraced in that way only brothers do. "Where are Mom and Dad?" I asked, glancing toward the house. "They went shopping," Tony replied, gesturing to the yard. "Come in. Put your bike over here." As I parked the bike, the warmth of family wrapped around me, grounding me in a way the open road never could. Another chapter of the day unfolded, steeped in memories, kinship, and the quiet joy of being home. The gate creaked faintly in the summer breeze as Dad's car pulled to a stop in front of it. With a quick press, he blew the hooter, the familiar sound carrying through the yard. A moment later, I came around the corner, the faint scent of oil lingering in the air.

From Hippie to Preacher

Dad's face lit up with a broad smile as he spotted me, and before I could say anything, Mom was already out of the car, hurrying towards me. "Sean!" she called, her arms wide open. We hugged tightly, her warmth bringing a wave of nostalgia. As we pulled apart, Dad drove the car inside, parking it neatly under the shade. "Sean, where are you coming from?" they both asked almost in unison. "Welkom," I replied casually, brushing a speck of dust off my shirt. "And Sophia? Where's she?" "With her parents," I said, grinning. "She's six months pregnant now." "Wow," Mom exclaimed, her eyes widening. Her hands flew to her mouth in delight. "Six months already? Time is flying!" We walked inside together, the house brimming with that comforting sense of home. Dad's gaze wandered immediately to the Kawasaki bike parked near the edge of the

## From Hippie to Preacher

garage. He raised a brow but said nothing for the moment. In the lounge, we settled into familiar spots. I let the conversation flow as if I'd never been gone. "We're living in Richards Bay now," I explained. "Orbit got a long-term contract there." Dad nodded approvingly. "That's good. Things are steady here too. I'm happy. Only working afternoon shifts now—2 PM to 10 PM. gives me plenty of time to relax in the mornings." Mom leaned forward, her expression shifting. "Have you heard about your sister? You're eldest?" I shook my head. "She's moved to Potchefstroom. Living with a guy who works there. I want them to get married, but you know how stubborn she is." I chuckled softly. "That sounds like her." "And your other sister, Antoinette" Mom continued, is driving buses in Pretoria now. It's a decent job, but she's far away."

# From Hippie to Preacher

Dad shifted in his chair, looking at me. "So, when are you heading back?" "Not tonight," I replied, watching Mom's face light up. "I'll leave tomorrow at two o'clock." The conversation shifted again. I leaned back in my chair, my thoughts drifting as I looked out the window. "I'm thinking of selling the bike," I said offhandedly. Tony, who had been silently listening, perked up. "What are you going to buy this time?" "Not a bike," I said with a grin. Tony snorted. "So you're not a hippie anymore?" Laughter rippled through the room, warm and unrestrained. It felt good to be back home, surrounded by family, the little threads of life weaving themselves back together again, if only for a night. Back at the caravan under the sprawling branches of the big tree, I took a deep breath, letting the evening's calm wash over me.

From Hippie to Preacher

The faint glow of little lights flickering in the other caravans nearby painted a picture of quiet contentment. The long, gruelling road trip and the whirlwind weekend were finally behind us. Sophia stood beside me, one hand pressed to her lower back, her head shaking in slow disbelief. "I'm not traveling again for a while," she said, her voice a mix of exhaustion and determination. "This was too much." I smiled and nodded, knowing she meant it. As I opened the caravan door, she stepped in and made a beeline for the bed, collapsing with a sigh that echoed her relief. Thankfully, her mom had packed us a feast of a lunch—so generous, in fact, that there was plenty left to turn into dinner. While Sophia rested, I began unpacking the car. Each bag, cooler, and stray item seemed heavier than the last, but the quiet hum of the night made the task bearable.

Once everything was stowed, I clicked on the kettle, the soft whistle promising a comforting cup of coffee to end the day. Dinner was simple yet satisfying, eaten under the cover of our tent. We savoured every bite while the world around us came alive with night-time sounds. Fruit bats flitted and dove just beyond the tent's edge, their silhouettes darting through the dim light. They were old companions now, their nightly routines as familiar as the rustle of leaves in the breeze. They lived in the trees that formed a natural shelter around us, their movements a reminder of how alive the world remained even in stillness. Sophia glanced up, a small smile playing on her lips. "There's no place like home," she said softly, her eyes taking in the caravan and the tent.

## From Hippie to Preacher

"Even if home is this." I chuckled, understanding exactly what she meant. Tomorrow, I'd be back to the grind, another day of long hours and hard work. But for now, we soaked in the peace, letting the quiet cradle us in its embrace. There was no rush. No deadlines. Just the two of us, the bats, and the night.

Work was the same, day in and day out, month after month. The rhythm of the construction site was predictable, the kind of monotony you didn't even notice after a while. But this Wednesday was different. It began just like any other, with the buzz of machinery and the smell of earth and grease in the air. Until my boss called me to the office. The office wasn't some polished, glass-walled structure. It was an old shipping container, planted like a tin box in the middle of the sprawling site. Other

# From Hippie to Preacher

containers, all identical in their rusted, weather-beaten exteriors, surrounded it like a makeshift fortress. They housed tools, spares, and every piece of equipment you could imagine. The setup wasn't just practical—it was tactical. The boss liked to keep an eye on everyone who came to collect something. Nothing got past him or Uncle Piet, our store man, who had an uncanny knack for knowing exactly where to find anything in that labyrinth of containers. I stepped up to the office door, wiping the sweat from my forehead. Inside, the boss barely looked up before pointing to the truck just outside the office. "Moodley will take you to the caravan," he said gruffly, as though this were any other errand. "Sophia's gone to the hospital. Ben"s wife took her. Hurry—she's in labour."

## From Hippie to Preacher

It took me a second to process. Labour? Sophia? My heart skipped a beat. Moodley, the driver, was already making his way to the truck, his pace as brisk and business-like as always. "Let's go!" he barked over his shoulder, not bothering to look back. "Thanks!" I shouted to the boss, though he had already turned his attention to a stack of papers on the desk. I jogged after Moodley, my boots crunching over the gravel as the reality of the situation sank in. Sophia, in labour. It wasn't just any day after all. It was the start of something entirely new. The van jolted to a screeching halt, the tires spitting gravel as the vehicle rocked forward. I steadied myself against the door, throwing a quick, "Thanks!" over my shoulder before leaping out.

From Hippie to Preacher

The air was thick with the metallic tang of coal dust and grease, a grimy reminder of the conveyor belt I'd been working on for hours. Inside the caravan, I grabbed my things, moving quickly. There was no time to waste. My skin felt gritty, coated in coal dust that had darkened me nearly to pitch black. At the ablution block, I scrubbed furiously under the warm stream of water, watching the soot swirl down the drain in inky rivulets. With fresh clothes on and a renewed urgency in my chest, I jumped into my battered Beetle, the engine sputtering to life as I sped off toward Empangeni. Richards Bay had no hospital of its own, and Empangeni, the neighbouring town, was our only option. The road stretched ahead. My knuckles were white against the steering wheel, my mind racing faster than the car. **Sophia. The baby.** I couldn't let my thoughts spiral; I just needed to get there.

From Hippie to Preacher

When I finally pulled into the hospital parking lot, I barely remembered cutting the engine. Inside, the fluorescent lights buzzed faintly as I rushed to the receptionist. She glanced at me with practiced calm, directing me to the maternity ward. My boots echoed down the sterile hallway as I broke into a run, my heart pounding against my ribs. Was I too late? The thought hit me like a punch as I arrived at the ward. A nurse, sensing my urgency, gestured for me to go in. Sophia lay on the bed, looking utterly exhausted but radiant. In her arms was the tiniest bundle, swaddled tightly. She smiled at me, her face lined with fatigue but glowing with a quiet joy. I leaned down to kiss her forehead, whispering, "Thank you." She beamed and gently turned the bundle toward me, revealing a delicate, scrunched-up face. "Little Sophia," she said softly, her voice filled with wonder.

## From Hippie to Preacher

I grinned, overwhelmed by a cocktail of pride and awe. Leaning in, I kissed her again, unable to tear my eyes away from the baby. This was her. **My daughter.** The weight of it pressed into my chest like a new kind of gravity. The nurse tapped my shoulder, breaking the moment. "You'll need to wait outside while we finish up," she said gently. Outside the ward, I found Ben's wife waiting. She had been the one who had brought Sophia here when it all began. I greeted her with heartfelt thanks, my voice still trembling with emotion. She gave me a knowing smile, her eyes kind. And just like that, I became a family man. I wasn't just me anymore—I was a husband, a father, a man with responsibilities far greater than I imagined. Ben's wife had asked me, just before she left, to send her congratulations and regards to Sophia. I thanked her again for bringing Sophia to the

hospital when it mattered most. Now, with Sophia and our new little one peacefully asleep. I found myself stepping into a moment of quiet, a rare pocket of time to think. But the matron interrupted that brief pause, her presence calm but firm. "You should come back tonight," she said. I nodded, my heart still caught in the whirlwind of the past hours. Driving back to the caravan park, my thoughts turned over a persistent worry. Could I let little Sophia grow up in a caravan, no matter how cosy we tried to make it? The answer weighed heavy and undeniable. No, I couldn't. It wasn't just about the space—it was about the stability, about building a home where memories could take root. The decision seemed to make itself. Before long, I found myself pulling into an estate agent's parking lot. "Good afternoon," the woman behind the desk greeted me. "How can I help?"

"I'm looking for an apartment to rent. Something available right away," I said. She scanned her list. "We only have one townhouse at the moment. It"s in Meer en See. Would you like to have a look? "Yes, that would be great." As I followed her car through the winding streets, a feeling of unease crept in. This was the first time I'd made a decision like this without discussing it with Sophia. It felt like uncharted territory, but the thought of providing for my family kept me moving forward. The townhouse stood at the end of a quiet street, bathed in sunlight. The air carried a strong sea breeze, invigorating and salty. The estate agent motioned to a spot for me to park, and I stepped out, taking in the surroundings. It seemed pleasant enough, but I couldn't shake the feeling of unfamiliarity.

From Hippie to Preacher

"This way," she called, already opening the front door. I followed her inside, unsure of what to expect—or even what I was looking for. "This is a cordon bleu chef's kitchen," she said brightly, motioning to the cabinets and countertops. To me, it looked like any other kitchen I'd seen. "Spacious lounge," she continued, leading me further in. The space seemed smaller than she made it out to be, not much larger than the tent we'd been calling home. "Here's the gorgeous bathroom." She gestured with a flourish, but it was an ordinary bathroom, nothing special. She pressed on, undeterred. "This is the main bedroom, and over here, an extra room. Very spacious." I looked around, trying to align her enthusiasm with what I saw. For a moment, I wondered if we were even in the same house.

# From Hippie to Preacher

"And the lock-up garage," she said, ushering me outside. "The owner removed the door because it was giving trouble, so no battles there!" She smiled like it was a selling point. She noticed my furrowed brow. "Do you like it?" she asked. "It's... fine," I replied cautiously. "What about water and electricity?" "Very affordable in this neighbourhood," she assured me quickly. "And it's all on the owner's name, so you save on connection fees." She rattled off more reasons why this townhouse was perfect, but my mind had already wandered. Could this place really be a fresh start for us? "I'll need to discuss it with my wife," I said finally. "Of course. Shall we set an appointment for you both to come by? How about 3 p.m. on Friday?" "That works," I said, shaking her hand.

From Hippie to Preacher

As I drove away, the salty sea breeze followed me, mingling with thoughts of Sophia, our little one, and the possibility of making this place more than just a building—a home. The warm glow of the evening lights outside the hospital room gave the small space a cosy, almost tranquil feeling. I sat close to Sophia, who cradled little Sophia in her arms, her soft smile full of tenderness. "She's so lazy to drink," Sophia murmured with a chuckle, tilting her head to watch the infant with amused affection. "Maybe she wants another flavour," I suggested, grinning. The idea was silly, but we giggled like teenagers sharing a secret. "When can you come home?" I asked, resting my hand gently on Sophia's arm. "The matron said Friday," she replied, her voice filled with the promise of returning to normalcy. "I can go home then."

# From Hippie to Preacher

"Great! I want you and our little princess to come check out the townhouse in Meer en See. I saw it this afternoon, and if you like it, we can move in." Sophia raised a brow, her smile teasing. "With what furniture?" I hesitated, my smile faltering for a moment, but then I pressed on. "The thing is, I don't want little Sophia growing up in a caravan." My voice softened, heavy with earnestness. "She deserves better. You both do." Sophia's expression melted into something gentler, her smile lighting up her face. "I want to come and see it. Thank you," she said quietly. I reached for her hand, giving it a soft squeeze. "My little princess must grow up normal," I said, and in a lighter tone added, "I brought you a chocolate. Maybe little Sophia will like chocolate-flavoured milk."

Sophia burst into laughter, her eyes sparkling, and the baby squirmed, making small, protesting sounds. "You've woken her now!" Sophia scolded playfully. "Maybe she *is* hungry. Pull the curtains around the bed so I can feed her." I did as she asked, drawing the curtains to give her some privacy. Sophia adjusted her gown, offering the baby her breast. Little Sophia latched on hungrily this time, her small hands clutching at her mother. I watched, enchanted by the scene, and quipped, "If you don't finish all your milk, no chocolate for you!" Sophia laughed, shaking her head. The baby made soft, contented noises as she drink, and for a moment, the world seemed to shrink to this small, perfect bubble of love and joy. The nurse peeked in, her voice soft. "Everything all right?"

# From Hippie to Preacher

"Yes, everything's fine," Sophia assured her with a smile. I stayed a while longer, making sure she didn't need anything else. "We've got everything in the bag I packed," I said. "Oh, and I almost forgot—Ben's wife, what's her name again? Shila?" "Yes," Sophia confirmed, her brow lifting in curiosity. "She sends her congratulations and said she'll visit tomorrow while I'm at work." "That's sweet," Sophia said, stifling a yawn. I kissed her softly on the forehead, then leaned down to plant a gentle kiss on the baby's head. "Goodbye, my loves," I murmured. Sophia looked at me with such pride that my heart swelled. She was radiant, even in her tiredness, holding our little girl as if its most precious gift. Friday, after collecting my pay, I made my way to the caravan to clean up. The coal dust clung to me like a second skin, a grimy reminder of the long hours spent at the tipplers where I

worked. I scrubbed myself quickly, the warm water biting at my hands, and hurriedly tidied the caravan for Sophia and our little one. The thought of seeing them warmed me more than any shower could. When I arrived at the hospital, Sophia was dressed and waiting, our baby cradled lovingly in her arms. Her eyes lit up as I walked in, and she smiled—a sight that never failed to make me feel as if I'd won some unseen lottery. I kissed her gently and grabbed the bag she had packed, while she carried our little princess, her movements careful and tender.

Sophia slid into the backseat, her voice soft but filled with excitement. "It'll be so good to go home," she said, though I knew her mind was already on the townhouse. "But first, we must go see it. Don't forget we have the appointment."

I nodded, steering the car toward the estate agent's office. When we pulled up, she gave me a look, part mischief, part joy. "I'm coming with you. Should I bring the papers?" she asked. "Yes, I think so," I replied, already sensing her anticipation. We followed the agent to the house, the car rumbling quietly as we approached the quiet street. Sophia glanced out the window, her smile widening. "I actually like this suburb," she said, her voice thoughtful. I parked the car, quickly stepping out to open the door for her. She climbed out carefully, our baby nestled close to her chest. We walked in behind the agent, the crunch of gravel underfoot giving way to the soft creak of the front door. The house smelled faintly of fresh paint, a promise of new beginnings. Sophia's eyes darted around the kitchen, and she smiled approvingly. "This is nice," she said. She moved through the lounge and into

## From Hippie to Preacher

the bathroom, nodding again. "This'll do fine." Then she stepped into the main bedroom, the sunlight pouring in through the windows. "This will catch the morning sun," she observed. She peeked into the spare room next. "It"s big enough for Little Sophia," she murmured, her voice tinged with a mother"s satisfaction. She inspected the lights, flicking a switch here and there, and then turned back to me with a shake of her head, a signal of her approval. It was more than I'd hoped for. "Great," the estate agent said, pulling out a set of papers. "Just fill in everything, and do you have the deposit?" "Yes," I said, setting the bag down. Taking the baby from Sophia, I let her handle the forms. I'd never been much good with paperwork, but she was quick and efficient, her pen flying across the pages.

# From Hippie to Preacher

In no time, the agent handed us the keys, the cool metal pressing into my palm with a weight that felt monumental. After the agent left, we lingered in the house, wandering from room to room as if to convince ourselves it was real. Sophia stood in the kitchen, rocking the baby slightly as she looked out the window. "It's going to be a good home," she said softly. And as I stood there, the weight of the keys in my hand and the sight of my family before me, I knew she was right. This was the start of something better. The sun hung low in the sky, casting its warm, golden light over the caravan park as we pulled up to our little home-on-wheels. The drive back had been uneventful, save for the detour at the Spar, where I'd grabbed a few meat pies for dinner. They sat on the passenger seat beside me, the warm scent of gravy and spices teasing my hunger.

From Hippie to Preacher

When we arrived, a small group of women stood outside near the caravan, chatting animatedly. Their conversation ceased the moment Sophia opened her door, stepping out with little Sophia cradled in her arms. "Oh, look at her!" one woman exclaimed, rushing forward. The rest followed, their faces lighting up as they cooed and fawned over our daughter. "She's beautiful!" said another, her eyes wide with admiration. Sophia's smile radiated pride. She stood tall as each of the women took turns holding our little girl for a brief moment, watching them like a hawk. Her gaze never left our daughter, her maternal instincts in full force. Then Ben's wife, Shila spoke up. "So, did you two take the house?" "Yes," we said in unison, the word spilling out in a shared excitement that made the women chuckle. Sophia added, "We'll need furniture now."

From Hippie to Preacher

Shila clapped her hands together. "I'll take you to OK Furniture tomorrow. Sometimes they have specials on all the basics. Beds, tables, chair—you name it." "That'd be perfect. Thanks so much," I said, genuinely grateful. With the pleasantries exchanged, we retreated into the caravan, ready to unwind. But the moment the door closed behind me, my nose crinkled. A sharp, unmistakable smell hung in the air."What's that smell?" I asked, half-suspicious, half-dreading the answer. Sophia looked at me with a knowing smirk. "It's little Sophia. She"s made a poo."I groaned inwardly. Back then, disposable nappies were a luxury—or perhaps not even a thing yet. We used washable nappies, and they required a bit of effort. Sophia set the baby down on the bed and began cleaning her with practiced hands, her voice low and sweet as she murmured to the baby.

"Sean," she said without looking up, "take that plastic tub and fill it halfway with water. I'll soak the nappy in it to wash tomorrow." I sighed, but I took the tub and went outside to the water spout. The night air was cool, and the sounds of the caravan park the distant hum of conversations, the bark of a dog—were oddly soothing. By the time I returned, Sophia was gently powdering the baby, her voice still soft and full of love. It was a side of her I never tired of seeing. "Thanks, Sean," she said, motioning to the tub. "Just leave it in the tent for now, but first, take this nappy and put it in there." I recoiled, eyeing the offending item she held out. "No way. You can put it in yourself. I'm not touching that thing." Sophia burst out laughing, the sound rich and unrestrained. "I've never seen a grown man so scared of a nappy!" she teased, her laughter filling the caravan.

# From Hippie to Preacher

I couldn't help but chuckle, albeit sheepishly, as I took the tub and set it down in the tent. Sophia's laughter was infectious, and soon, I found myself grinning despite the ordeal. The caravan smelled faintly of baby powder now, a comforting scent that mingled with the love and warmth of our small, perfect family. This was life—a little messy, a little smelly, but full of moments that made it all worthwhile. The Saturday sun bore down on the yard, filtered only slightly by the thin cloud cover, as I stood in the container office with the site manager. It smelled of diesel and distant metal grinding, a scent I had grown used to. I adjusted my cap and leaned against the battered desk, glancing out at the sprawling industrial site. "I'll be moving out of the caravan soon," I said, the words carrying a sense of relief. "Maybe by next weekend. We've found a townhouse in Meer en See."

# From Hippie to Preacher

The site manager, a burly man with a perpetually furrowed brow, looked up from his clipboard. "Good news," he said, nodding. "Take next weekend off so you can clean out the caravan. I'll let Head Office in Welkom know. They can send the new boilermaker here—we could use another pair of hands." I smiled, grateful for the understanding. "Thanks, boss." "Just remember," he added, his voice gruff but not unkind, "you'll work the following weekend when you were supposed to be off. Fairtrade." "Fair enough," I said, tipping my cap as I stepped outside. The wind had picked up, carrying the fine black grit of coal dust that clung to everything it touched. I made my way to the conveyor belt project I was working on, the structure slowly taking shape under my hands and the efforts of the team.

# From Hippie to Preacher

By the time we knocked off at 4 p.m., I was covered in a layer of soot and grime that clung stubbornly to my skin, a second skin of the job. Back at the caravan, the sight of Sophia waiting for me melted the fatigue of the day. Her smile was radiant as she greeted me with a kiss, then pressed a finger to her lips. "Shhh," she whispered. "Little Sophia is sleeping." I nodded, grinning, and grabbed my bag to head to the ablution block. The sticky coal dust seemed to resist every scrub, but the warm water felt heavenly, washing away the day's toil. By the time I returned to the caravan, a steaming cup of coffee and a plate of ginger biscuits awaited me on the table in the tent. Sophia sat there, her face glowing in the soft light, a look of excitement playing on her features. "I have good news," she said. "Tell me," I replied, sinking into the chair and feeling the weariness of the day ebb away.

## From Hippie to Preacher

Her smile widened. "We have furniture," she said, her eyes sparkling. "It'll be delivered Monday morning. Sheila's coming with me to oversee it. I even got ready-made curtains." "You've been busy," I said, taking her hand and giving it a gentle squeeze. "What all did you get?" "A fridge, a double bed, a single bed, and a pinewood lounge suite," she rattled off, her words bubbling with enthusiasm. "Not too bulky. Oh, and a washing machine and a small stove." I blinked, impressed. "Wow. Where'd you get all the money for that?" "My husband is working," she teased, her eyes twinkling with humour. "I used his money." We both laughed a sound that filled the small caravan with warmth. Sophia's happiness was infectious, and for the first time in a long while, I felt like life was finally falling into place.

# From Hippie to Preacher

The promise of a proper home, a space for our family, and the simplicity of a shared coffee under the canvas roof of the tent made my heart feel full. Life was good—dusty, gritty, and unpredictable—but undeniably complete. The truck rumbled to a stop at the caravan park's boom gate, its tired engine groaning as the brakes squealed in protest. Darkness had already settled across the sky, the glow of the caravan park's scattered lights casting long, uneven shadows over the dirt paths. Moodley leaned out of the driver's window, nodding at the guard as we gathered our things. This was the routine. He dropped us here every evening and picked us up again in the mornings. No private vehicles were allowed on the work site it was company policy. One by one, we jumped off the truck's flatbed, boots crunching on the gravel. The familiar smells of cooking fires and damp grass filled the air

## From Hippie to Preacher

as we headed toward our respective caravans. It was always the same at this hour: men shuffling off to clean themselves of the grime that clung stubbornly after a long day's work. Murmurs of conversation in the air, a baby crying somewhere in the distance. Sophia stood in the shadows by the tent near our caravan, her slim figure faintly illuminated by the yellow glow of the nearest lamp post. She was shaking the pram, a second-hand gift from one of the kind women here. The wheels squeaked softly as she moved it back and forth. When she spotted me, her face lit up, and she started pushing the pram in my direction. We kissed briefly, her free hand brushing against my cheek. "Hurry," she said, her voice filled with excitement. "There's something I want to show you." I raised an eyebrow, intrigued. "Good news?" I asked.

# From Hippie to Preacher

"You'll see," she said, giving me a playful push. I wasted no time, heading straight to the showers to rinse off the layer of black dirt and sweat that clung to my skin. The hot water was a welcome relief. I scrubbed away the grit, watching it swirl down the drain until I finally felt human again. When I returned, my little Sophia—our daughter—was awake, her tiny fists flailing as she let out a soft coo. She was nestled in the carrycot, her round face peeking out from the folds of a hand-knitted blanket. I scooped her up gently, cradling her close. She looked at me with wide, curious eyes, her small fist jammed into her mouth as if deep in thought. I grinned and played a quick game of peek-a-boo, covering my face and then revealing it with exaggerated expressions. She made strange noises in response, her tiny sounds full of wonder.

# From Hippie to Preacher

Sophia, her mother, reached for her. "Let me hold her," she said, smiling as she took the baby from my arms. She laughed as she cradled our daughter, her voice lilting with affection. "Dada doesn't like you making a poo, does he?" she teased, wrinkling her nose as if to drive home the point. I chuckled and backed away, letting them have their moment. Watching them together made something tighten in my chest—not in pain, but in a warm, quiet way that reminded me why I worked as hard as I did. This was for them. The scent of baby powder lingered heavily in the caravan as Sophia's call pulled me from my thoughts. "Sean, put the pram in the car. We're ready to go to the new house." Her voice was light but carried a note of excitement. "Aha, so that's where we're headed," I said, teasingly. She climbed into the backseat, cradling little Sophia gently in

her arms. Her face glowed, the kind of tired but fulfilled glow that only a new mother could wear. "Can you grab the baby bag from the tent, please?" she asked her voice soft. I ducked back to the tent, rummaging until my hand found the familiar weight of the bag. With a quick shove, I placed it on the passenger side and slid behind the wheel. The dark road ahead stretched out in quiet, flanked by whispering palm trees swaying in the breeze. A sense of relief washed over me. One of these days we are going to leave the cramped caravan life behind, stepping into something new and permanent. I pulled up in front of an open garage. No door, but it would do. The house loomed behind it, shadows playing across the fresh paint. As I stepped out, I held the car door for Sophia. She smiled, shifting the baby in her arms. "The house keys are in the side pocket of the baby bag," she

said. With a quick rummage, I retrieved them, locking up the car before following her inside. The first thing that hit me was the smell— home-cooked food, warm and inviting. My stomach growled audibly. "Wow," I muttered. "Is this the right place?" Sophia turned her smile radiant with pride. "It's our home," she said simply. Inside, the space was like a dream. The furniture was arranged perfectly, curtains hung neatly, and the small details— vases, picture frames, the little touches that made a house a home—were all in place. My jaw slackened as Sophia laid the baby in the carrycot and moved to the oven, her movements graceful despite her exhaustion. "Did you do all of this?" I asked, incredulous. She turned and grinned. "With a little help from Shila," she admitted. "The food was done about an hour before your knock-off time."

From Hippie to Preacher

I whistled low as I wandered into the bedroom. The bed was made, its covers crisp and fresh. I opened the cupboard, half expecting it to be empty, and let out another whistle when I saw our clothes hanging neatly. The spare room was just as orderly. "You've outdone yourself," I called, shaking my head in amazement. Back in the kitchen, she had set the small breakfast nook with plates and utensils. We sat down to steaming pork bangers, creamy mash, and a side of peas. "We're sleeping here tonight," Sophia announced between bites. My eyes widened. "Are you sure?" She nodded. "Everything from the caravan is here. Towels, cups, coffee—you name it." "But my work clothes—" "They're still at the caravan. You'll just have to change there in the morning and leave the car over there," she said, catching the frown forming on my

## From Hippie to Preacher

forehead. "Don't worry. Shila and Maggie are coming over tomorrow to help me finish unpacking." I relaxed at her reassurance, letting the warmth of the meal and the soft hum of the house settle into my bones. This wasn"t just a house—it was home. And for the first time in a long while, it felt like we were truly starting anew. A few months later while the evening sun cast a golden hue through the windows as little Sophia crawled across the living room floor, her determined focus fixed on her dummy. She"d tossed it just out of reach and now pursued it with a giggle. That made my chest tightens with joy. I laughed so hard my eyes brimmed with tears, marvelling at how the tiniest things could feel so monumental. "Seven months," Sophia said softly, her voice carrying that mix of wonder and disbelief. She stood by the kitchen counter, wiping it with a dish towel. "Seven

months in this house already." I nodded, watching our daughter wrestle her prize back into her mouth, the soft rubber smeared with drool. "The best decision we ever made," I agreed. "Imagine her doing that outside the caravan—dummy in the dirt, stones in her tiny hands." My stomach twisted at the thought, but Sophia only smiled, her gaze far away. "Mom"s going to be over the moon when she sees her on Friday," she said, her smile widening. "They'll be here for a whole week." "Lucky for them, lucky for us," I said, leaning back in my chair. "Can't believe I'm actually on leave for once. Usually, we'd never get the chance—not with the company closing every December." Sophia raised an eyebrow. "And you're actually okay with this? You? Mister „never takes a day off"?" "Well," I admitted, grinning sheepishly, "the timing couldn't be better.

# From Hippie to Preacher

The bonus and my salary came through right before they arrived. And it's not like I had a choice—the boss said the rain's delayed the contract, so we all have to take turns with the three weeks leave. Besides," I added with a shrug, "it"s a chance to breathe." Sophia chuckled, shaking her head. "You? Breathing? I'll believe it when I see it." Later, as the light outside softened into dusk, I slipped on my shoes and announced, "I'm heading to Spar. Need anything?" She shook her head, busy clearing the table. I grabbed my wallet and headed down the road. Halfway to the store, a white van caught my attention, the bold *Bell Equipment* logo glinting on its side. My pace slowed, deliberately, as I scanned the area for the driver. By the time I reached the store, I spotted him climbing back into the vehicle. My pulse quickened, and I dashed toward him, calling out. "Hey, mate! Quick question—are

# From Hippie to Preacher

Bell Equipment hiring boilermakers?" The man paused, his hand on the door handle, and gave me a once-over. "Actually, yeah," he said. "We're expanding." "Thanks," I said, my mind already racing. Walking home, with the pies I started piecing together how I'd break the news to Sophia. The company offered housing allowances, and if I could get in, we might finally afford to buy this place outright. No more rent. No more worry. The aroma of warm meat pies and golden chips filled the house. I set the food on the table and turned to Sophia. "You know," I began, "we should talk about Bell Equipment. They're hiring, and— hear me out one of the perks is housing allowances. We could actually buy this place." Sophia didn"t answer immediately, her hands busy placing the plates. "And when the contract's done?" she asked, her tone careful. "We'd have to go back to Welkom. Do you

really want that?" I leaned closer, brushing my hand against hers. "No, I don't. And I don't think you do either." She sighed, soft and tired, taking a bite as she mulled it over. "Let me sleep on it," she said at last. I nodded, lifting little Sophia from the floor and settling her on my lap. The pies were almost gone, but I swiped a finger across the last streak of sauce on my plate and offered it to her. She hesitated, scrunching her face in suspicion, but soon enough, her tiny finger found its way to the plate. "Sean!" Sophia scolded, laughing. "What are you teaching our girl?" We chuckled together, and the tension melted away like steam rising from the plates. Whatever tomorrow held, at least we had this moment—our family, our home, and the small, beautiful chaos of it all. The sun hung lazily over the beach, its warmth tempered by a brisk wind tugging at our umbrella. "Sean,

# From Hippie to Preacher

Sophia is calling—just push the umbrella deeper into the sand," she urged, shielding her eyes from the sun. I nodded, set the cooler box down, and helped Sophia steady the umbrella before the gusts could carry it away. Nearby, Sophia"s mom cradled the carrycot with practiced care while her dad wrestled with a roll of canvas. After a few minutes of chaotic teamwork, everything was in place: the umbrella firmly anchored, towels spread out, and snacks within easy reach. Sophia knelt beside our little one, the baby's delicate skin protected by the highest SPF sunblock she could find at the pharmacy. She applied it carefully, her hands moving with a mother"s precision. I noticed she took no shortcuts with herself either, her arms and legs glistening with lotion. We could smell the nostalgic banana-coconut scent from far.

# From Hippie to Preacher

"Come on!" her dad called out to me, already jogging toward the waves. The promise of body surfing was irresistible. We plunged into the surf, the water shockingly cool against the warm afternoon air. The rhythm of the waves became our playground, each swell a new challenge to ride. Sophia's mom lingered by the shoreline, her feet sinking into the wet sand as the cool water swirled around her ankles. She watched us with an amused smile, her hair catching the wind. When we finally emerged, salt-streaked and exhilarated, Sophia handed me the baby. "Can you take her to the water"s edge? Let her feel the waves," she asked, adjusting the long-sleeve vest that shielded our daughter from the sun. I carried our little one down to the shore, her small body a warm, wiggling bundle in my arms. The sand yielded beneath my feet, and I found a spot just far enough from the advancing tide.

# From Hippie to Preacher

I set her down gently. She giggled as the cool water tickled her toes, her tiny hands eagerly digging into the wet sand. But the sea has its own plans, and just as I turned to call Sophia over, a larger wave pushed forward. I scooped our daughter up as the water reached her shoulders, the salty spray dampening her curls. She blinked in surprise but didn"t cry. I brought her back to Sophia, who had been watching from her towel, soaking in the sun. "Everything okay?" she asked, already holding a towel out for the baby. "All good," I replied. We settled back into the rhythm of the afternoon, snacking on chips and sipping cold Cokes from the cooler the wind began to pick up, the fine grains of sand stinging our legs as the afternoon wore on. It was the kind of wind that Richard's Bay was famous for— unrelenting until the cool of evening set in.

From Hippie to Preacher

With little Sophia now fast asleep in her carrycot, we decided to pack up. The walk back to the car was quiet, the baby"s peaceful face a small reminder of how perfect the day had been, sandblast and all. And just like that the weak was gone. Thank you for everything. Sophia"s mom said they kissed gently, the kind of kiss that lingered even after it was over, and then I shook Sophia's parents" hands firmly. We watched them as they drive away, their car growing smaller until they disappeared around the corner. The moment they were out of sight, Sophia darted inside toward the spare room, her soft laughter echoing faintly through the house.

I sank into the lounge chair, my thoughts wandering back to the conversation I'd had with Sophia's dad two evenings ago.

# From Hippie to Preacher

"There's a mine captain who wants to buy my Kawasaki 1300," He'd said, leaning forward. "He'll pay any price." "I already know what price I want," Sophia's dad had raised an eyebrow, his expression intrigued. I'd continued, sliding the papers across the table to him. "Just make sure he deposits the money into the bank before you hand over the bike." There was something thrilling about it all—a plan forming, clear as day in my mind. I'd had my eye on a snow-white beach buggy for a while now. It wasn't just any buggy; it was the kind of vehicle dreams were made of. With that buggy, the three of us could cruise along the beach together, wind in our hair, freedom at our fingertips. This was back when driving was still allowed on the beach—a time that already felt like a distant memory. "Sean, Sean!" Sophia's voice pulled me back to the present. "What are you dreaming about so

early in the morning? And with your eyes wide open!" She laughed her voice bright and teasing. I chuckled, shaking my head at my own foolishness. The faint scent of baby powder wafted through the air, grounding me. "Is everything alright?" I asked, watching her carefully as she folded a towel in her hands. "Yes," she said with a soft smile. "I cleaned her up and gave her a bottle. She'll be awake in about an hour. I've got her sleeping routine figured out." "Great," I said, standing and stretching. "Would you like a Coke?" "Tea, please," she replied, surprising me. "Tea?" I echoed, raising an eyebrow. "Are you sure? "Yep," she said with a definitive nod. "You're not… pregnant, are you—" I started to tease, but before I could finish, she flung the towel at me, her laughter bubbling over. "Don't be ridiculous!" she said, shaking her head and smiling in that way that made my heart feel

lighter. The house felt peaceful, quiet in a way that had been rare after the past busy week. It was just the three of us again— Sophia, the baby, and me. The rhythm of our little family settled around us like a warm embrace. As I lay on the bed, little Sophia perched on my chest, her chubby fingers clutching at my shirt with determination; I felt the sweet warmth of contentment. Her giggles filled the room as I playfully wiggled my fingers in front of her, her wide eyes following every move. Then, with a flourish, the curtains were drawn back, flooding the room with sunlight. "Come on, Mr Lazy Man," her mom teased, standing in the doorway with a knowing smirk. "It's your last day of leave. Get up; breakfast is ready." Before I could protest, she reached down and scooped Sophia into her arms. The baby"s protests were instant and loud—her little fists flailing, her bright

## From Hippie to Preacher

eyes filled with betrayal. She wanted to keep playing with her dada. But her mom was undeterred, setting her gently into the well-worn baby chair we'd acquired from a kind woman at the caravan park before we moved out. As I pulled out a chair at the dining table, I couldn't help but reflect on how fleeting these moments were. Tomorrow, the rhythm of family life would change again. Last night, as we lay in bed, we"d talked about the immediate future—the kind that feels urgent and heavy when you've got bills to pay and a baby to feed. I'd decided to stick with my current job at Orbit, where the hours were gruelling, but the pay was too good to walk away from just yet.

Three weeks of leave had flown by like sand slipping through my fingers. We'd had lazy days filled with simple pleasures—my in-laws

joined us for a week, we drove aimlessly through quiet roads, and we let ourselves indulge in takeouts far more than we should. Even Sophia had gotten a break from the kitchen, though she didn't seem to mind much. It had been a time of small joys, of fleeting moments that seemed insignificant but felt monumental now, as the last day loomed. Sophia's impatient grunts broke through my thoughts. She twisted in her chair, her chubby hands reaching out as if to demand freedom. Her pouty lips quivered with frustration. "All right, little one," I murmured, grabbing a dab of marmalade on my finger. I held it out to her with a grin. She opened her mouth and Her reaction was instant—her eyes narrowed, her tiny face contorted in dramatic offense, and she spat the jam out with such vigour that it dribbled down her chin.

# From Hippie to Preacher

I couldn't hold back my laughter as her mom shot me a look of mock reproach. "Don't worry, sweetheart," she cooed at Sophia, dabbing her chin with a napkin while suppressing a smile. "Daddy won't do that again, okay?" But the baby wasn"t convinced. When I jokingly offered another marmalade-covered finger, she shook her head with theatrical disapproval, her tiny arms flailing as if to ward off the offending treat. I chuckled and surrendered, licking the marmalade off my own finger as Sophia's mom raised an eyebrow at me. "Ok" I said with a wink. The morning is full of laughter and stolen moments of affection. As the sunlight streamed through the kitchen window, illuminating Sophia's toothy grins and her mom's exasperated smile, I knew this was the memory I'd hold close. My last day of leave looked promising, indeed.

From Hippie to Preacher

The afternoon sun hung golden in the sky as I stopped in front of the back door, my pay packet tucked snugly in my pocket. Sophia stood at the door, her silhouette framed in sunlight, holding the hand of our little one— our miracle, already two years old. I stepped out of the car, taking a deep breath as the invigorating scent of salty sea air filled my lungs. Time had slipped by so fast it felt like a dream, but there she was, real and vibrant, pointing her tiny finger at me with wide, curious eyes. She turned to her mom, her voice as soft and clear as a bell. "Dada," she announced with pride, her grin as bright as the sky. Sophia smiled down at her, repeating the word, "Dada," like it was the sweetest refrain. The little one wiggled free, her intent clear: she wanted to run to me. My heart surged with love, but I held up a hand. "Not yet, sweetheart," I murmured, glancing at my

grimy work clothes. She hesitated, confused, until I bent down and kissed her cheek, leaving a smudge of dirt. I leaned over and kissed Sophia too, who didn"t seem to mind the faint streak I left on her. "Come inside," she said, stepping back to let me through. I made my way to the bathroom, peeling off the day's labour. The hot water felt like a second skin, washing away the grime and the fatigue, leaving me fresh and whole again. Sophia called from the other side of the door, her voice teasing. "I have a surprise for you, but first, finish cleaning up." When I finally emerged, hair damp and clean-shaven, I felt like myself again. I flopped down on the couch beside her, the cushions sighing beneath us. She gave me a sly smile. "So, you want to know the news?" I stretched lazily. "What news?" "Your mom and dad are coming to visit." "That's great!" I said, sitting up

straighter. "I haven't seen them in ages." "And they're bringing Tony and his wife with" she added with a laugh. "Even better," I said, grinning wide. Then she hesitated, a glint of mischief in her eye. "That"s not all," she continued. "Paul and his wife are coming too." I blinked. "All at the same time?" "Yep," she said, clearly enjoying my reaction. "Wow." I leaned back, shaking my head. "Where is everyone going to sleep?" She gestured around the room, already full of toys and laundry baskets. "Your parents can have our room. We'll take the spare. The rest..." she waved at the couch, the floor, and anything else soft, "...will have to figure it out in here." We both burst out laughing, imagining the chaos that awaited us. "I haven't met Paul's wife yet," I said, suddenly thoughtful. "What if she's one of those who walk around with her nose in the air?"

# From Hippie to Preacher

Sophia grinned. "Oh please. People from Vanderbijlpark aren't snobs. Now, if they were from Potchefstroom..." She trailed off, raising her eyebrows, and we both dissolved into laughter. The little one toddled over, her tiny face lighting up with the purest joy at our mirth. "Hehahe," she squealed, trying to mimic us, her giggles unrestrained. That was it—the cherry on the cake. Tears of laughter streamed down our faces as we clutched our sides, the sound of our child's innocent glee filling the room like music. "What a Friday afternoon," I said, wiping my eyes. Sophia was curled up beside me, holding her belly as if to contain the laughter. The little one tried again to copy her mother, tumbling over with a squeal. And in that moment, nothing else mattered. The world could wait. Life, in all its beautiful, messy glory, was here in this room, wrapped up in laughter and love.

From Hippie to Preacher

The warm glow of a Saturday morning filled the house with an almost magical energy. Little Sophia, all giggles and boundless joy, had already claimed her spot on the bed, tugging at Oupa's mustache with her tiny fingers. Their laughter was a melody of its own, drawing amused chuckles from my mother, who watched their antics from the doorway. Her eyes sparkled with the kind of love only grandparents know. For me, this day was a rare treasure. A day off from work, given to spend with my family. I had made plans to make it count. Early morning, we'd hit the beach, and by afternoon, the coals of the braai would be glowing, promising good food and even better memories. The kitchen was alive with activity. Tony's wife hummed softly as she brewed coffee for everyone, the comforting aroma curling through the air. Sophia was meticulously packing the cooler

# From Hippie to Preacher

bag with drinks and snacks, her brow furrowed in concentration. The extra basket was soon filled with goodies, and I loaded it into the boot alongside the beach umbrella and the large canvas we'd lay out on the sand. Tony had taken charge of the deck chairs, packing them neatly into his car, his efficiency as reliable as ever. With steaming mugs of coffee in hand and slices of toast disappearing from plates, we gathered in the living room. Conversations flowed freely, each one reflecting on the wonderful week we'd spent together. They praised Sophia for her hospitality, a warm glow of pride spreading across her face. Today was the last day of their visit, and though tomorrow would bring goodbyes, the day ahead was still ours to enjoy. The house buzzed with final preparations. The unmistakable scent of sunblock—banana and coconut—filled the air

as Sophia knelt by Little Sophia, carefully rubbing it onto her sun-kissed cheeks. Everyone followed suit, the ritual a small but vital part of our beach-bound adventure. The familiar smells mingled with laughter, creating a sensory memory we'd carry long after the day was done. Soon, with the cars packed and the spirit of adventure ignited, we were ready to go. The beach awaited, and with it, my promise to spoil them all with ice cream as the waves lapped at our feet and the sun danced on the horizon. This was family—a messy, joyful, perfect moment in time. Time waits for nobody, and it was hard to believe that five years had passed since we left Welkom, embarking on what was supposed to be a two-year contract. Now, with Orbit's agreement with RBCT finally concluded, the end felt both sudden and long overdue.

# From Hippie to Preacher

The farewell gathering was held at the Bay Hall, a cosy venue nestled near the harbour. It was there that everyone saw Sophia again— our little Sophia, now five years old and a bundle of life, a mirror of the years that had quietly slipped away. The company had gone all out: caterers served tender lamb on the spit, music wafted through the air as a DJ spun old records, and the bar, wide open and well- stocked, became a hub of cheer. All of it was generously paid for by the company—a fitting send off for years of hard work. After the speeches were delivered and the bonuses handed out, the atmosphere turned festive. Drinks flowed freely, and soon the dance floor came alive with contractors and their wives swirling to the music. Laughter filled the room as couples lost themselves in the rhythm, their steps as light as their hearts, and the joy showed no signs of slowing.

# From Hippie to Preacher

At our table, the boss and his wife joined us, their presence easy and familiar. His focus, however, was fixed on little Sophia, who sits nearby talking to the other children, blissfully unaware of the weight of the conversation. "Please," he said, turning to my wife with a touch of urgency, "talk to Sean. Convince him to come back to Welkom. He mustn't leave us now. There's a future with us, and we don't want to lose him." She shook her head gently but firmly. "We've made up our minds," she replied, her voice steady. "We're staying in Richards Bay. Next year, Sophia starts school. We're happy here." The boss leaned in and whispered something to her. I couldn't catch the words, but I saw her shake her head again, smiling faintly. "Thank you," she said, "but I know."

Later, as we sat eating, the memory of that whispered exchange lingered. Curiosity got the better of me. "What did he say?" I asked, keeping my voice light. She smiled a touch of warmth in her eyes. "He said you can come back anytime in the future. He'll take you immediately." I smiled, too, the weight of the moment settling into something sweet. As the sun began to set, its golden hues dancing on the water's surface. I felt a quiet contentment. I had stuck it out till the end, and as I looked at my family and the life we had built, I knew it had all been worth it. The morning sun filtered through the curtains, casting warm patterns on the floor. I stretched and glanced at Sophia, her face calm but focused as she sipped her tea and wrote something in her notebook. Since I stopped working, life had felt...unmoored, like a ship adrift. I knew I needed to find direction soon, but Sophia's suggestion the night before

had given me something to look forward to. "Visiting the family sounds perfect," I'd said, relieved at the thought of reconnecting before little Sophia started school and before I had to dive back into the grind of a new job. But, of course, Sophia had plans. "We can't just leave on a whim," she had replied, her voice carrying that practical tone I knew so well. "We need to organize a few things." "Like what?" I had asked, grinning as I poured me and little Sophia each a Coke. Little Sophia, sitting cross-legged on the couch with a book far too big for her age, perked up at the sound of the bottles opening. "Packing, for one," Sophia began, ticking off a mental list. "And phoning everyone to make sure it's alright to visit." Now, as I stood by the car, cleaning out the remnants of sand from our last trip to the beach, her words echoed in my mind. Living in Richards Bay had its perks—warm weather,

## From Hippie to Preacher

endless beaches—but the fine grains of sand seemed to infiltrate every corner of life, especially the car. The old rubber mats held on to the beach like a jealous lover. I shook them out with a firm thwap against the pavement, grinning as memories of the past flitted through my mind. The car—a second-hand Mercedes—gleamed faintly under the morning light. It wasn"t new, but it was sturdy, reliable, and had become a symbol of compromise and progress. Three years ago, we'd traded in the VW Beetle and the cash from selling my Kawasaki 1300 for it. I could still hear the heated argument Sophia and I had when I'd nearly bought a Beach Buggy instead. "You're a father now," she'd said, hands on hips, her piercing gaze brooking no argument. "No more toys. We need something practical."

## From Hippie to Preacher

And she was right, of course. She always was. Now, the Mercedes was more than a car; it was a part of our family. Little Sophia loved climbing into the back seat with her backpack full of toys, while big Sophia appreciated its automatic transmission for errands. I still missed the thrill of the bike sometimes, but I couldn't deny how good it felt to drive this car, practical yet elegant. I chuckled, imagining the looks I'd get if I drove into the mining village in this car. Me—the long-haired dreamer they'd once dismissed as a useless hippie—rolling up in a Mercedes. Would they even recognize me? Maybe I should make a detour there on our way to visit family. It would be good for a laugh. For now, though, there was work to do. I grabbed the vacuum from the garage and set to clean the interior, whistling a tune as I went.

Nearby, little Sophia giggled, her Coke forgotten on the table as she chatted with her mother. Life felt...lighter, and freer, and I realized this trip might be just what we needed—a chance to reconnect, to show the people we loved that we were still here, thriving in our own way. The dawn's early light still lingered in the air as we rolled through Empangeni, the gentle hum of the road beneath us a lullaby for little Sophia. She had drifted off to sleep on the back seat, her tiny body curled like a question mark. Sophia—her mother—turned back, her arm reaching to adjust the makeshift pillow beneath her daughter's head. Careful hands smoothed down a blanket as best as they could in the cramped space, ensuring the little one would rest comfortably for the journey ahead. By the time we reached Harrismith, the world outside was wide awake, and so was little Sophia.

# From Hippie to Preacher

Her sleepy eyes now sparkled with curiosity as we pulled into the petrol station. Sophia excused herself to take the child to the restroom while I filled the car. The rhythmic clicking of the fuel pump was a small reminder of our progress before I found a shaded spot to park. They re-joined me, and together, we made our way to the Wimpy for breakfast."I'm glad we left home at five," I said, almost to myself, as we settled into the red-cushioned booth. Morning light poured through the large windows, glinting off the cutlery. Little Sophia sat next to her mother, her tiny fingers flipping through the menu pages as though she were reading a story. She pointed to a picture of a massive burger, her excitement bubbling over. "This one!" she announced, her small finger tapping the glossy image. Sophia laughed softly, brushing a strand of hair from her daughter's face. "That

one's a bit too big for you, my love. How about we get you a normal burger instead, with a milkshake?" Satisfied with the compromise, little Sophia nodded eagerly. The waitress, dressed in the classic red-and-white uniform, took our order with a smile. While the girls shared their moment, I savoured the scent of freshly brewed coffee, letting it mingle with the warmth of bacon and eggs that soon arrived on my plate. Around us, other patrons were engrossed in their meals, forks and knives clinking against plates. It was a simple scene, but it carried the comforting weight of routine—a pocket of peace before the long road ahead. After breakfast, I excused myself to the restroom, stepping into the cool stillness of the tiled corridor. By the time I returned, the girls were ready, little Sophia holding her mother's hand tightly. "Next stop, Bethlehem," I announced with a grin as we

## From Hippie to Preacher

climbed back into the car. The road ahead seemed to stretch endlessly, its lanes now bustling with weekend travellers. Friday traffic wasn't forgiving, and I murmured, "We shouldn't do this again on a Friday." Sophia nodded in agreement as we cruised forward, our Mercedes gliding through the warm midday air. Blessings come in many forms; I thought as I adjusted the speed control and turned up the air conditioning. No need for open windows or the sticky heat that clung to older cars. Little Sophia perched on her knees in the back seat, her bright eyes peering out the rear window. Every passing car seemed to hold a story she wanted to know. When one zoomed by, she waved enthusiastically, her tiny hand a burst of energy against the glass. Now and then, a passing driver would respond with a cheerful honk or a kind smile.

From Hippie to Preacher

Her joy was infectious, spreading from the back seat to the front. As the world rolled by in streaks of green fields and blue skies, I couldn't help but feel grateful—for the journey, for the company, and for the quiet magic of moments like this. The streets of Welkom stretched out before us, both familiar and strangely foreign, like a long-lost photograph distorted by the years. The golden sunlight spilled over the low, faded houses, catching on the patches of gravel and streaks of dust that lined the cracked roads. It felt as if the town itself had aged with time, its once-proud façade weathered and softened by neglect. Sophia sat beside me in the car, her arms folded loosely, her gaze fixed outside the window. A small, resigned sigh escaped her lips, barely audible but heavy with unspoken thoughts.

# From Hippie to Preacher

"This place," she murmured, her voice soft yet tinged with something bitter. I said nothing, keeping my eyes on the road as we slowed to a stop in front of my in-laws" garage. The corrugated metal door stood unchanged, its rusted edges defying the years, though the peeling paint on the adjacent walls revealed patches of bare, grey concrete beneath. I could almost hear Sophia's silent reflection: *did I really grow up here?* I tapped the horn. The sharp sound echoed down the still street, startling a stray dog that scurried into the shadows. "Well," I muttered, half to myself, "here we go." We stepped out of the car, the heat of the sun pressing against us like an old, familiar cloak. Moments later, Sophia's mother appeared at the door, a bright smile lighting her face as she stretched her arms wide. "You're early!" she exclaimed, crouching as little Sophia dashed into her

embrace. The sight of their reunion softened Sophia's expression, and for a moment, the tension dissolved into something warmer. We exchanged greetings, hugs all around, as the air filled with the buzz of family reunion. It wasn't long before Sophia's father arrived with Mark and his family in tow. Mark's booming voice broke the quiet. "Sean! Look at you now," he bellowed, gesturing dramatically toward my car. "Driving a Mercedes-Benz, huh? You are getting smart!" He turned to Sophia, enveloping her in a bear hug and planting a kiss on her cheek. "And you," he teased, "is he treating you well?" Sophia smiled, playful and assured. "Spoiled," she replied with a wink. Mark laughed, and soon the atmosphere was alive with chatter and movement. Suitcases were hauled from the car, with Mark helping to carry them inside at Sophia's mother"s instruction.

## From Hippie to Preacher

"Put it in the spare room," she called over her shoulder as she guided little Sophia toward the kitchen. Inside, drinks were offered, and the children quickly bonded, their laughter echoing through the house as they darted around in endless games of tag. Darlene, Mark's wife, was quiet at first, her smile tentative amidst the boisterous conversation. But Sophia, ever the diplomat, drew her into a gentle chat, and before long, they were talking as though they'd known each other forever. The easy rhythm of the evening gave way to its share of surprises. Over dinner, Sophia's father raised an eyebrow at me. "I hear you're out of a job," he said bluntly.

"The mine's looking for boilermakers." I shook my head. "Thanks, but no. We're happy in Richards Bay."

## From Hippie to Preacher

The topic shifted, and the next day, Saturday, brought a much-anticipated braai at the in-laws' house. It turned out to be a perfect day, the smoky aroma of grilling meat mingling with laughter and shared stories. As the sun dipped low on the horizon, Sophia's father leaned back in his chair. "You should stay the week," he suggested, his tone warm. I shook my head with a smile. "No, tomorrow we're heading to Potchefstroom for a day, then Vanderbijlpark. By next Monday, we'll be back home." The promise of the road ahead loomed, but for now, we were here—held in the embrace of family and fleeting moments that would linger far longer than the time spent.

The sun was busy setting behind us as we get closed to Richards Bay, casting long shadows that stretched ahead like the lingering

## From Hippie to Preacher

memories of our trip. The cool coastal breeze whispered a welcome, its salty tang washing over me, but my mind wandered back to the family we had visited. Little Sophia had thrived in the whirlwind of attention from relatives, her laughter a melody that followed us wherever we went. Dad and Mom, now living near the railway line in Potchefstroom, seemed content. Dad had left the mines and taken up work on the railways, a quieter yet no less industrious life. Nights there were filled with the rhythmic clatter of passing trains, the sound weaving through our dreams as if we were passengers in motion. The day we arrived, Little Sophia stood at the front gate, mesmerized by the trains rumbling past. She waved enthusiastically, her joy erupting in delighted jumps and squeals whenever the drivers waved back.

From Hippie to Preacher

In Vanderbijlpark, our time was brief. Paul managed only two hours with us before duty called him back to his gruelling 12-hour shifts at Iscor. Though fleeting, those moments were precious. We spent the nights at Tony and Helleen's house, where a serene calm enveloped everything. It felt like a sanctuary. Little Sophia bonded quickly with her cousins, while Helleen and my wife, Sophia, struck up a friendship that seemed destined. Tony, ever the entertainer, relished the opportunity to braai, and the warm gatherings around the fire remain etched in my memory—a celebration of family and simple pleasures. Now, as we neared home, the familiar sights of Richards Bay brought a sense of relief. The long road had lulled Little Sophia to sleep on the backseat; her head nestled on the side. Sophia rested too, leaning against the window, the soft strains of East Coast Radio filling the car.

From Hippie to Preacher

I slowed to a stop outside the house, and as if on cue, they both stirred awake. Sophia yawned deeply while Little Sophia clambered out, announcing her urgent need for the bathroom. I opened the car door for her, and then the back door of the house, she ran inside, her small feet pattering down the hallway into the shadows. Sophia stepped out of the car, stretching her back with a contented sigh. "There's no place like home," she said her voice soft with gratitude. She walked ahead, flicking on the lights one by one, their warm glow pushing back the approaching night. I lingered outside for a moment, inhaling deeply. The cool, salt-laden air was a sharp contrast to the smog of Vanderbijlpark. It felt like a cleansing, a homecoming in every sense. That night, as we lay in bed, the events of the past week unfolded between us in quiet conversation. We spoke of the joy of

reconnecting with family and the bittersweet moments along the way. I couldn't help but share my disappointment as we passed through Blyvoor the mining village where I had grown up. The house of my childhood stood neglected, the streets echoing years of abandonment. Even the workshop where I had apprenticed as a boilermaker was unrecognizable; I was a stranger in a place once so familiar. Sophia gently reminded me that the old club where I'd spent lively evenings had long since closed its doors. It was a place lost to time, much like the village itself. But our home, our sanctuary by the sea, awaited us. Sophia smiled and declared our bed the most comfortable in the world, and I had to agree. The comfort of familiarity wrapped around us as we drifted to sleep, our hearts full from the journey yet glad to be back.

From Hippie to Preacher

The week's memories replayed in our dreams, a bittersweet symphony of family, change, and the enduring solace of home. Tuesday evening was a turning point. After much discussion, we decided I should explore a job opportunity at RM Engineering. The setup was nearly identical to Orbit Engineering, a company I was familiar with. The biggest advantage? RM Engineering didn't require the frequent travel that had worn me down at Orbit. By Wednesday morning, my decision was firm. After breakfast, I packed my big wooden toolbox and the smaller carry-around toolbox into the trunk of the Mercedes Benz. I wanted to be prepared in case they asked if I had my own tools. The day was overcast, with a gentle drizzle that gave everything a fresh, vibrant look. Sophia and her mother decided to join me for the ride, eager to see what the day would bring.

From Hippie to Preacher

The rainy weather seemed to breathe life into the landscape, making the drive serene and almost poetic. When we reached RM Engineering, the sounds of grinders and hammers filled the air as I pulled up to the gate. It was a symphony of industry, and I couldn't help but hum Neil Diamond's *"What a Beautiful Noise"*. Leaving little Sophia and her mother in the car, I grabbed my folder of papers and walked toward the office. The air smelled of fresh wood and metal, like a forest meeting a workshop. Inside, I approached the reception desk. The woman behind it was older but radiated warmth with her kind smile. Flowers adorned the space, their colours softening the industrial vibe. I asked if they needed a boilermaker, and she gestured for me to sit down as she made a call. "Mike will be here shortly," she informed me.

# From Hippie to Preacher

A few moments later, a man emerged from a side door. He wasn't dressed in overalls like I'd expected, but in neat business attire, exuding an air of quiet authority. He reminded me of an English gentleman with a stiff upper lip. Approaching with an outstretched hand, he introduced himself "Mike," he said. "Sean," I replied, shaking his hand firmly. He motioned for me to follow him, and we entered his office. The space was immaculate, more like a banker"s office than a workshop manager's. As soon as we sat down, he asked for my papers. His expression brightened the moment he saw Orbit Engineering on my résumé. "You worked for Orbit Engineering?" he asked, smiling ear to ear. I nodded, and his questions came in quick succession was I married? Where did I live? Did I have reliable transportation? I answered them all, and he seemed genuinely pleased. After taking my

papers, he left the room, leaving me to wait. Time dragged each moment feeling like an eternity. Finally, Mike returned, still smiling. "Because you've worked at the RBCT coal terminal, we want you over there," he announced. "Have you ever met Albert?" "Yes," I said. "I know him very well. He's the foreman there." "Correct," Mike replied. "You'll be working closely with him. I'll give you a temporary car permit for tomorrow. From Thursday, you can carpool with Albert. The hours are 7 to 5, with work every second weekend. Do you accept these conditions?" I nodded, and we signed the necessary papers. Mike handed me a gate pass for the next day, and just as I was about to leave, he added, "Oh, and one more thing—we pay monthly, with a 15% housing allowance." I couldn't suppress my smile as I left the office. I felt a sense of accomplishment as I climbed back

into the car. Sophia looked at me curiously. "Did you start working already? Did you forget about us in the car?" Before I could respond, little Sophia piped up. "Dada, did you forget us?" We all laughed, the tension of the day dissolving in that moment. I started the car, still smiling. "Are you taking the tools back home?" Sophia asked, frowning slightly. "Yes," I said, pulling out of the parking lot. Her disappointment was palpable as she gazed out the window. "Only for today," I explained. "I'll need them tomorrow at RBCT." Her eyes widened. "You're going back to RBCT?" "Yes," I confirmed. "That's great!" she exclaimed. "You loved working there!" I smiled again. "The hours are good— 7 to 5—and I"ll only work every second weekend. Plus, there's a housing allowance." Sophia clapped her hands in excitement. "We need to celebrate!" she declared. Little Sophia

joined in, shouting, "Yippee! Milkshakes for everyone!" As we drove off into the rainy afternoon, the future seemed brighter, filled with promise and possibilities. The road ahead felt smooth, and for the first time in a long time, life looked as rosy as the flowers in the RM Engineering office. The sun filtered through the curtains, casting soft morning light across the breakfast table. Sophia, her blonde curls bouncing as she climbed onto her chair, looked up at her mom with bright eyes. "Mom," she began, carefully balancing a piece of toast in her hand, "can we pick up Elise? She's coming with us to the beach today." Her mom smiled, sipping her coffee. "That won't be a problem. Which friend is this, Sophia?" Sophia tilted her head and rolled her eyes as if the answer should be obvious. "Oh, Mom! Elise! She's been my best friend since first grade."I chuckled, folding the newspaper in front of

me. "Mmm and just how are we getting to the beach today?" Sophia turned to me, a mischievous glint in her eye. She shrugged dramatically and then grinned. "You're going to drive us, Dad." Her confidence was contagious, and her mom and I burst into laughter. After breakfast, we piled into the car and swung by Elise's house. Sophia leaned out the window to chat with Elise's mom, gesturing animatedly about our plans. "We'll be back by three o'clock," she assured her. Elise waved and shouted a cheerful goodbye as we drove away, her excitement matching Sophia's. At the beach parking lot, I took charge. "All right, everyone! Grab something

and let's get set up." "I carried the cooler box and canvas. We also had two sun umbrellas and deck chairs to set up." Sophia and Elise raced ahead, their arms laden with towels. They managed to plant the beach umbrella

firmly in the sand and spread their towels underneath. The air was soon filled with the warm, tropical scent of coconut and banana as the girls rubbed sunscreen onto each other's shoulders, giggling. As they sprinted to the waves, I settled into my deck chair, sunglasses in place, and sighed. "I can't believe she's already ten," I said to my wife, shaking my head. "She's growing up so fast," my wife agreed, adjusting her sunhat. "What a blessing it is to live here by the coast. Just think of the families inland—they'd have to save up and plan for a trip like this." Sophia had already confided earlier in the week that she wanted to invite Elise to church tomorrow. It was one of the best decisions we'd made as a family, joining the community church. The warmth and fellowship of the congregation felt like a second home. "Did you know," Sophia asked, breaking my reverie, "that Albert is studying

to become a pastor?" "No," I said, surprised. "He's never mentioned it, and we travel to work together every day." Before I could dwell further, the girls came racing back from the water, their laughter bubbling like the surf behind them. Sophia, dripping and carefree, held out a Coke. "Mom said to ask if you want one." I nodded, and she handed it to me, grinning as if she'd just accomplished something heroic. Watching her, a thought crossed my mind, something I hadn't considered before. Maybe I could study to become a pastor, too. Perhaps tomorrow, I'd ask at church about enrolling. I imagined myself preaching on my off weekends, giving back to the community that had embraced us. The girls had returned to the beach towel, chatting and drawing pictures in the sand. Sophia suddenly spotted the ice cream vendor. "Mom! Can we get ice cream?"

From Hippie to Preacher

My wife glanced up, shading her eyes from the sun. "Let's see what he has." We each picked a treat, savouring the cool sweetness under the warm sun. For a moment, life felt as perfect as the rhythmic crash of waves against the shore. Monday, drive home from work, was quiet, the late afternoon sun casting a warm glow across the horizon. I drummed my fingers against the steering wheel, replaying Albert's words in my mind. He'd suggested something that resonated deeply: a regular Wednesday evening Bible study, alternating between his place and ours. "Great idea," I had said without hesitation. With my studies to become a pastor well underway, dedicating time to share the Word seemed not only right but necessary. The course was a serious commitment: two years of rigorous study, followed by another two years of practical training—preaching sermons, conducting

funerals, and counselling families through life's storms. It wasn't just about learning scripture; it was about living it, embodying it in every moment. And now, with Albert's idea, it felt like another layer of purpose had been added to my routine. Life had taken on a rhythm—a blend of work, study, and faith. Every second weekend was dedicated to church, and when the weather allowed, we would find solace on the beach, the waves a reminder of God's unending grace. Sophia, my wife, was flourishing in her own walk of faith. She had joined the women's cell group, which had quickly become her sanctuary of fellowship. Mornings often found her and the other women at the hospital, bringing comfort to patients with kind words and prayers. Her compassion inspired me daily.

From Hippie to Preacher

At home, everything had subtly, yet profoundly, changed. Mealtime prayers became a sacred ritual; before each meal, we bowed our heads, giving thanks for the food and the hands that prepared it. Mornings began with a shared prayer, a protective blessing for little Sophia and me as we stepped out into the world. Evenings closed with prayers of gratitude, whispered together before the day's worries melted into rest. These simple acts of devotion grounded us, reshaping the fabric of our lives. Living as Christians was meant to live—it wasn't just a phrase anymore; it was our reality. And with that shift came other changes. Our circle of friends evolved, too. The community of believers we found welcomed us with open arms, their warmth and shared purpose a balm for our souls. Finding the Lord Jesus had not only saved us but had also set us on a new

# From Hippie to Preacher

path, one filled with clarity, intention, and love. Each day felt like a gift, a reminder of the transformation happening not just within us but in every aspect of our lives. The sun was just beginning to warm the December morning as little Sophia bounded into the kitchen, her excitement bubbling over like a pot on the stove. "It's my last day at primary school, Mom!" she announced, her face glowing with a mix of pride and nerves. "Next year, I'm going to high school!" Her mother smiled warmly, setting down a plate of toast. "I can't believe it. My little girl all grown up," she said, a trace of wistfulness in her voice. Before little Sophia could respond, the shrill ring of the telephone interrupted the moment. With a little squeal of delight, she jumped from her chair and dashed to answer it.

From Hippie to Preacher

"Hello! Ouma?" she chirped, her face lighting up even more. "Yes, it's my last day today! Thank you. Love you so much!" She paused, listening, and then called out, "Mom, it's Ouma Potch. She says hello!" Little Sophia's excitement was infectious as she handed the phone to her mother and twirled back toward the table. By the time breakfast was nearly done, my wife had joined us at the table. Her expression was bright as if she had been saving some special news. "Sophia," she began, looking at her daughter and then at me, "I have something wonderful to share. Your grandma and grandpa are on their way here. They'll be staying for a week!" Little Sophia gasped, her hands flying to her mouth. "Really? Grandpa too?" Her mother nodded. "Yes, your Grandpa is retiring. The railway decided it was time, especially with his health not being what it used to be. They're halfway

here already." I smiled gently. "They'll be here for Sunday, in time to hear my first preach. It'll be quite a start into this new chapter of life." Sophia's heart swelled with pride and anticipation. "Your first practical sermon," she whispered, as though savouring the words. The family stood together then, offering a moment of gratitude to the Lord for the blessings that seemed to overflow on this day of endings and beginnings. As the clock ticked closer to school time, little Sophia grabbed her bag, gave her parents quick hugs, and dashed out the door. Eager to cherish every precious moment of her final day at primary school, she lingered, soaking it all in. Then, it was time for me to go. As Albert sounded the hooter, the kitchen fell silent once more. Yet, the quiet carried a different tone—one of hopeful anticipation, brimming with the promise of a bright and exciting future ahead.

From Hippie to Preacher

The sun was sinking low on the horizon, casting long golden shadows as I climbed out of Albert's bakkie. The faint crunch of gravel under my boots was drowned out by the sight that greeted me—my parents' car, parked neatly in front of the garage. A jolt of excitement rippled through me, followed by warmth. They had mentioned they were coming. "Hello, Dad! Ouma and Oupa are here!" Little Sophia's voice rang out, her words tumbling over one another in excitement. She was perched comfortably between her grandparents on the stoep, a little queen holding court. Her eyes sparkled as she turned to them, soaking in their undivided attention. I waved and greeted everyone warmly before excusing myself. The dust from the work clung to my skin, and a shower beckoned. As I stepped into the bathroom, Sophia my wife padded in, carefully balancing

a clean set of clothes in her hands. little Sophia wants to go to Elise for the night. Her mom called, and they're going to play CDs." "That's fine, love she can go," I replied. Later that evening, after a leisurely chat, Dad leaned back in his chair and looked at me. "What about fish and chips for supper?" "That sounds great," I agreed, already imagining the smell of fried fish and vinegar-doused chips filling the kitchen. With little Sophia off to Elise's house for the night, the evening carried an unhurried simplicity. After dinner, we gathered for a quiet moment, bowing our heads in prayer. It wasn"t something my parents were used to, and I could feel their eyes on me when I spoke the words aloud. When I finished, Dad broke the silence. "Since when did you start praying?" I looked up and met his gaze, smiling softly. "Since we were saved," I said simply.

# From Hippie to Preacher

For a moment, they exchanged glances. Neither said a word, but the weight of their curiosity hung in the air. Without another word, we all retired to our respective rooms, the quiet hum of contentment settling over the house like a blanket. Sunday morning dawned crisp and bright, the kind that made everything feel sharper and more vivid. "Little Sophia, who had spent the night at Elise's house, was dropped off early to get ready for church."Arriving at the church, the grounds were already teeming with cars, their polished exteriors gleaming under the sun. I scanned the rows, my gaze settling on Albert's car. Perfect. I steered into the spot directly behind him, figuring he wouldn't mind. Dad sat in the passenger seat beside me, a quiet, steady presence. In the backseat, Sophia sat with her hands folded neatly, betraying none of the tension I felt simmering under my skin.

# From Hippie to Preacher

We hadn't told my parents about today— about *me*—about the fact that this Sunday morning, I would step up to the pulpit for the first time. Not a word. Even little Sophia had been sworn to secrecy, and by some miracle, the child had kept her promise. Inside the church, people were already settling into their usual places, the familiar hum of greetings and whispers filling the air. We found an open spot near the back, enough for Sophia, little Sophia, Ouma, and Oupa to squeeze in. As everyone shuffled into their seats, Dad turned to me, his brow furrowing. "And where are you going to sit?" he asked, his voice tinged with curiosity. "Don't worry, Dad," I said, managing a weak smile. "I'll find a place."Sophia reached for my hand just before we stepped inside, her fingers squeezing mine in a silent reassurance. She leaned in close, her whisper soft yet steady. "Everything will be

# From Hippie to Preacher

Fine." Her kiss brushed my cheek, a fleeting touch of warmth and faith, and then she moved toward the pew with the others. I lingered for a moment, gathering myself, and then, heart thudding in my chest, I walked toward the front. The aisle seemed impossibly long, stretching out like a runway under a thousand watching eyes. My palms were damp, the distant murmur of voices growing muffled under the weight of my own thoughts. Albert was already sitting up there, his face pale but calm, though I could see the tension in his jaw. Our eyes met briefly, and he gave me a small, nervous smile. I took the seat beside him, trying to mirror his smile though my nerves were as raw as his. The congregation quieted. The service was about to begin, and soon, it would be my moment. My first preach. My first step into something

## From Hippie to Preacher

I had dreamed of for so long but never truly thought I'd reach it. And here I was. The sanctuary was filled with the gentle murmur of the congregation, a sense of anticipation hanging in the air after the final announcements. The head pastor stepped forward, his voice steady yet warm as he addressed the assembly. "Today, I'm not preaching," he began, eliciting a few surprised looks. "Instead, we have two student pastors here with us this morning. This is their very first time delivering a message, so I ask for your patience and encouragement." His gaze swept the room as he continued, "First up is Albert." The head pastor stepped down from the podium and walked over to take the seat Albert had just vacated. Albert, a young man with a nervous but determined expression, stood and approached the pulpit. He adjusted the microphone slightly, clearing his throat as

he faced the crowd. "Good morning, everybody," Albert began, his voice trembling just enough to betray his nerves. "If I look nervous, it's because I am nervous." The congregation laughed warmly at his honesty, the tension in the room easing. Albert smiled, clearly relieved that the ice was broken. "Let's turn our Bibles to Acts chapter 8, starting at verse 37," he said, waiting as pages rustled throughout the sanctuary. "And Philip said, "If thou believest with all thine heart, thou mayest." And he answered and said, "I believe that Jesus Christ is the Son of God." And verse 38, "and he commanded the chariot to stand still: and they went down both into the water, both Philip and the eunuch; and he baptized him." Albert paused, his hands gripping the edges of the pulpit. His eyes scanned the congregation, his confidence seeming to grow as he began to expound on

the passage. "Brothers and sisters," he said, "here in this passage, we see that belief is not the end but merely the beginning. Philip didn't just say, "If you believe, you will be saved." No, the final act of belief had to fulfill the truth of that belief. And so, Philip went with the eunuch into the water." Albert leaned forward slightly, his voice firm now. "Why, you might ask? To immerse him. That's what baptism means — to immerse. For those among us who have yet to fulfill this commandment of our Lord Jesus Christ, I urge you to do so. Don't delay. Remember, it's not enough to sprinkle a few drops of water on someone's head and call it done. You must be immersed. This act is a testimony of faith, an outward declaration of the inward transformation." "Amen," he concluded, stepping back from the pulpit. There was a murmur of agreement from the congregation, followed by polite

## From Hippie to Preacher

applause as Albert descended from the stage, his face flushed but glowing with accomplishment. The head pastor rose to his feet again, a proud smile on his face as he nodded at the young preacher. Albert took his seat, breathing deeply, his hands trembling slightly, but his heart full. The church was alive with the hum of murmurs and shifting pews as the head pastor stepped up to the pulpit. His voice carried with authority, resonating through the congregation. "The next pastoral student is Sean," he announced, motioning with a gentle wave. "Please come up." The murmuring swelled a mix of curiosity and subdued surprise. I raised from my seat, feeling the eyes of the congregation on me, their anticipation thick in the air. As I approached the pulpit, my nerves were tangible. But I knew humor was a bridge, and so, with a steadying breath, I addressed them:

# From Hippie to Preacher

"It's not me that's shaking," I said, a wry smile tugging at my lips, "it's my pants!" Laughter rippled through the room, breaking the tension. The smiles I saw gave me strength. I looked out over the rows of familiar faces, each a thread in the fabric of our community. "Good morning," I began voice steady now. "Let us all turn to Mark 16, verse 16. „He that believeth and is baptized shall be saved, but he that believeth not shall be damned." I paused to let the words settle, their weight undeniable. "Brothers and sisters, here we read the words of our Lord Jesus Christ. Jesus did not say that belief alone is enough. No, Jesus taught that baptism must follow belief. The complete act of faith is to believe and then to be baptized. This is an act of obedience, a symbol of surrender. And here, too, is a warning from our Lord: "If you don't believe, you are damned." These words,

# From Hippie to Preacher

spoken by Jesus after His crucifixion, carry a grave truth. "Yes, Jesus shed His blood for us, and yet He calls us to take this step of faith— to immerse ourselves in water as a sign of our transformation. Thank you, and Amen." I stepped back from the pulpit, my heart pounding as the congregation burst into applause. It wasn't for me, I reminded myself. It was for the truth of the Word. The head pastor returned to close the service with a prayer, and soon, we were outside, the crisp air filled with the warmth of congratulations. Members of the congregation greeted Albert, my fellow pastoral student, and me with firm handshakes and kind words. "You both did great," they said, their smiles genuine. The head pastor himself approached, his voice filled with pride. "Sean, Albert—you're going to make a great team."

# From Hippie to Preacher

What the outside world didn't know was that none of us pastors—including the head pastor—received salaries. We all worked jobs outside the church, serving not for profit but out of love and calling. As my family approached, little Sophia was the first to reach me, wrapping her tiny arms around my waist. "It was beautiful," she said, her eyes sparkling with innocence and pride. "Thank you, sweetheart." I bent to kiss her forehead. My wife stood a step behind me, her smile radiant as the sun. She pulled me into an embrace, her voice a whisper in my ear. "Congratulations." "Thank you," I said, holding her close, her warmth steadying me. Mom was next, her eyes shining as she spoke, her words a melody of pride. "I am so proud of you, Sean. Wait until I tell the whole family!" "Thank you, Mom," I replied, my heart swelling with gratitude.

# From Hippie to Preacher

Finally, my father stood before me, his hands trembling slightly as he grasped mine. His eyes glistened, and his voice was thick with emotion. "Sean," he said, pausing to gather his words, "you've come so far from being a hippie to becoming a preacher.

Well done, son." We embraced the kind of hug that speaks of history, redemption, and unconditional love. "That sounds nice," Sophia piped up, her voice chiming like a bell. "From hippie to preacher." And we all laughed together, the sound weaving into the fabric of a day I would never forget.

> "God the Father, God the Son, and God the Holy Spirit deserve all the praise and honour for making this book possible."

www.ingramcontent.com/pod-product-compliance
Lightning Source LLC
Chambersburg PA
CBHW051542010526
44118CB00022B/2552